# WORKBOOK

## HARCOURT SCIENCE

**Harcourt School Publishers**

Orlando • Boston • Dallas • Chicago • San Diego

www.harcourtschool.com

Harcourt

# Contents

Harcourt

# Reading in Science

Reading is very important in your becoming an independent learner—in being able to find, understand, and apply the information you need in the classroom and in your life. In science reading you are expected to find information, learn the meanings of scientific words, and put together ideas and observations. You can be helped in this reading and understanding by using the following suggestions.

To help you locate topics in *Harcourt Science* and most other science texts, use the:

- table of contents,
- titles of units, chapters, and lessons,
- headings and subheadings,
- index.

Look for and read these parts of a lesson in *Harcourt Science* to locate main ideas and other key information:

- Vocabulary Preview
- Investigate activity
- Process Skill Tip
- Find Out
- ✓ questions
- Picture captions
- Inside Story
- Summary
- Review
- Links
- Features

To help you recognize and read for specific kinds of information:

1. Recognize the text structure by looking for signal words
   - compare/contrast—*however, but, some, different, instead, on the other hand, like, unlike, both, neither*
   - sequence or how-to—*first, second, next, then, last, finally,* or the use of numbered steps
   - cause/effect—*since, because, as a result*

Harcourt

2. Preview the material to see at a glance which material you already know something about and which contains new or unfamiliar topics.

3. First, read the questions at the end of a lesson or chapter. Then read the lesson or chapter to find the answers. Also use the **Find Out** statements to help you identify what you need to find out while reading.

4. Construct graphic organizers or use the graphic organizers provided in the workbook to help you remember key points as you read.

5. Read the Science **Process Skill Tip** in each investigation to help you understand the meaning of a process skill. Do the Process Skill Practice page in the workbook for more information.

6. Write a summary of the main ideas of a lesson. Put in your own words (paraphrase) what you read about. Then compare your summary to the lesson summary in the book.

7. Look for comparison words such as *like* or *similar to*. These words can help you to understand something new by comparing it to something you already know about.

8. Read the entire sentence and sometimes the sentences around highlighted vocabulary to tell you what these words mean.

9. Make an outline of what you read to record main points.

10. Ask questions as you read. Write facts in one column on a sheet of paper. Write your questions in the column next to the facts.

11. Reflect on what you read. Write notes not only about what you read, but also about what you think, and why.

12. Use the **Review** in the text and the **Concept Review** and **Vocabulary Review** in the workbook to help you prepare for the chapter test.

Harcourt

# Chapter 1 • Graphic Organizer for Chapter Concepts

## Classifying Living Things

### LESSON 1
### CLASSIFYING

Why Classify

_____
_____
_____

The Five Kingdoms

1. _____
2. _____
3. _____
4. _____
5. _____

### LESSON 2
### CLASSIFYING ANIMALS

Animals With Backbones are

Called _____.

Examples

1. _____
2. _____
3. _____

Animals Without Backbones

are Called _____.

Examples:

1. _____
2. _____

### LESSON 3
### CLASSIFYING PLANTS

Two Groups of Plants

1. _____
2. _____

Harcourt

# Classifying Shoes

## Materials

shoes

newspaper or
paper towels

## Activity Procedure

**1** Take off one shoe and put it with your classmates' shoes. If you put the shoes on a desk or table, cover it first with newspaper or paper towels.

**2** Find a way to **classify** the shoes. Begin by finding two or three large groups of shoes that are alike. Write a description of each group.

**3** **Classify** the large groups of shoes into smaller and smaller groups. Each smaller group should be alike in some way.

**My classification:** 5     pop out    ones _____

_____

_____

**4** Write a description of each smaller group.

**My descriptions:** _____

_____

_____

_____

_____

**5** Stop classifying when you have sorted all the shoes into groups with two or fewer members.

Harcourt

Name _____

## Draw Conclusions

1. What features did you use to **classify** the shoes? _____

_____

_____

2. **Compare** your classification system with a classmate's system. How are your
   systems alike?

_____

_____

_____

   How are they different? _____

_____

_____

3. **Scientists at Work** Scientists **classify** living things to show how living things
   are alike. Why might it be important for scientists to agree on a set of rules for

   classifying living things? _____

_____

_____

_____

_____

   **Investigate Further** **Classify** other groups of things such as toys, cars, or pictures
   of animals. Write a brief explanation of your classification system.

_____

_____

_____

Harcourt

Name _____

Date _____

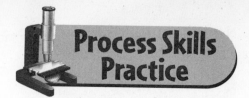

# Classify

When you classify living things, you group them based on similarities.
Things with many similarities may be classified in more than one way.

## Think About Classifying

Observe these pictures of shells. Classify the
shells into two or more groups. Fill in the
chart to describe your classification
system. Then answer the questions.

| Characteristic Used for Classifying | Name of Group | Shells in Group |
|---|---|---|
| Spiked | | 2 |
| semectrical | | 9 |
| Closed | | 4 |

1. Look at the shells in each of your groups. How could you classify the shells in
   each group into smaller groups? _____

   _____

   _____

   _____

2. Compare your classification with that of a classmate. How were your
   classifications similar? How were they different? _____

   _____

   _____

Harcourt

Name _____

Date _____

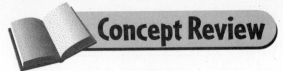

# How Do Scientists Classify Living Things?

## Lesson Concept

Scientists organize living things so they can be easily studied and discussed.

## Vocabulary

**classification** (A6)  **kingdom** (A7)  **moneran** (A7)  **protist** (A7)

**fungi** (A7)  **genus** (A8)  **species** (A8)

**Answer the questions below.**

**1.** Fill in the missing information on the chart about living things.

| The          Kingdoms | | |
|---|---|---|
| **Kingdom** | **Important Characteristics** | **Examples** |
| Animals | Many celled, feed on other | Monkeys, birds, frogs, fish, and spiders |
| Plants | Many celled make own food | Trees, flowers, ferns, and mosses |
| Fungi | Most many-celled, absorb food from other living things | Mushrooms, mold, Yeast |
| Protists | Most one celled make own food or feed on living things | Algae, amoebas, and diatoms |
| Moneran | One-celled, no cell nuclei; some make their own food, some feed on living things | Bactira |

**2.** The white oak tree has the scientific name *Quercus alba*. This is also the name

of the _Speices_____. What genus does the white oak belong

to? ___Quercus_____ What kingdom does the white oak tree

belong to? __Plants_____

*living things*

Harcourt

# Building a Model Backbone

## Materials

chenille
stem

wagon wheel
pasta, uncooked

candy
gelatin rings

## Activity Procedure

**1** Bend one end of the chenille stem. Thread six pieces of wagon-wheel pasta onto the stem. Push the pasta down to the bend in the stem. Bend the stem above the pasta to hold the pasta in place.

**2** Bend and twist the stem. What do you see and hear? _____

_____

**3** Take all the pasta off the chenille stem except one. Thread a candy gelatin ring onto the stem, and push it down.

**4** Add pasta and rings until the stem is almost full. Bend the stem above the pasta and rings to hold them in place.

**5** Bend and twist the stem. What do you see and hear? _____

_____

**6** Draw pictures of the model backbones you made. **Compare** your models with those shown in the picture on page A25.

Harcourt

Name _____

## Draw Conclusions

1. A real backbone is made of bones called vertebrae (VER•tuh•bree) and soft discs that surround the spinal cord. What does each part of your final model stand

   for? _____

   _____

   _____

2. How is your final model like a real backbone? _____

   _____

   _____

3. Study your final model again. What do the soft discs do? _____

   _____

   _____

4. **Scientists at Work** Scientists **use models** to study how things work. Would a piece of dry, uncoooked spaghetti work better than a chenille stem to stand for the spinal cord in your model? Explain your answer. _____

   _____

   _____

   _____

**Investigate Further** Think of other materials you could use to **make a model** of a backbone. Plan and make the model. Does it show how a real backbone works better than the model you made in the investigation? Explain.

_____

_____

_____

_____

_____

Harcourt

Name _____

Date _____

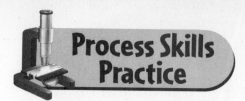

# Make a Model

You don't always need to see the whole thing to understand how part of it works. Models can be built to help you see just one part of a thing.

## Think About Making a Model

Todd wanted to show his younger sister Rebecca how a frog leaps. He decided to make a poster to show the leaping movements of a frog. He found a book with pictures of a frog leaping. The book showed that when a frog leaps, it makes six basic movements.

First the frog crouches down, bending all its legs. Then its feet and legs move straight out away from its body, pushing the frog away from the crouched position. While in midair, it pulls its front legs back to its sides and leaves its hind legs straight. Right before the frog lands, it puts its front legs in front of itself. The frog lands on its front feet first. Then it pulls its back legs toward its body and puts them on the ground.

1. Why would it be hard to understand the movements by just watching a frog leap? _It will be hard becuse it is hoping to qwkly._

2. Why do you think Todd made a poster instead of a working model of a frog?
   _Becuse a model can only be one at a time._

3. Do you think Todd's poster was a model? Explain. _No becuse a model is a 3D Demential and a poster is 2D pimntinal_

4. Besides Todd's poster, what other ways could Rebecca use to learn about how a frog leaps? _You could use a video camra_

Harcourt

Use with page A11.

Name _____

Date _____

# How Are Animals Classified?

## Lesson Concept

Animals are classified by whether or not they have a backbone.

## Vocabulary

**vertebrate** (A12)   **mammal** (A12)   **reptile** (A12)   **amphibian** (A12)

**invertebrate** (A13)   **arthropod** (A13)   **mollusk** (A13)

**Fill in the missing information on the charts.**

| Group | Important Characteristics | Examples |
|---|---|---|
| andins | Have moist skin and scales; begin life in water | Frogs, Tod |
| birds | Have wings and feathers; lay eggs | Eagles, owls, chicen |
| fish | Have scales; spend their entire lives in water | Salmon, trout and Flounder |
| Mammals | prodves milk for young | Cats, dogs, and peple |
| Reptiles | dry skin scales | Lizards, snakes, |

| Group | Important Characteristics | Examples |
|---|---|---|
| Mollusks | Have jointed legs | Crabs, insects, saarpino |
| Arthorpos | May or may not have hard outer shell | Clams, snails, Squids |
| Worm groups | | Earthworms, flat-worms, and |

Harcourt

Name _____

Date _____

# Plant Stems

## Materials

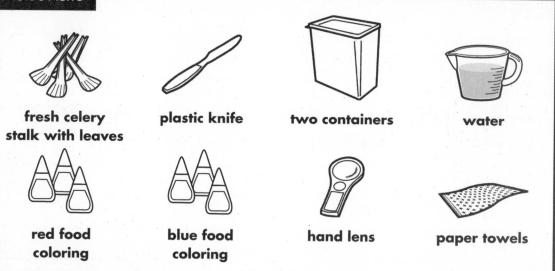

fresh celery stalk with leaves

plastic knife

two containers

water

red food coloring

blue food coloring

hand lens

paper towels

## Activity Procedure

**1** Use the plastic knife to trim the end off the celery stalk. Split the celery from the middle of the stalk to the bottom. Do not cut the stalk completely in half.

**2** Use the chart below.

**3** Half-fill each container with water. Add 15 drops of red food coloring to one container. Add 15 drops of blue food coloring to the other container.

**4** With the containers side by side, place one part of the celery stalk in each container of colored water. You may need to prop the stalk up so the containers don't tip over.

**5** **Observe** the celery every 15 minutes for an hour. **Record** your observations on your chart.

**6** After you have completed your chart, put a paper towel on your desk. Take the celery out of the water. Cut about 2 cm off the bottom of the stalk. Use the hand lens to **observe** the pieces of stalk and freshly cut end of the stalk.

| Time | Observations |
|------|--------------|
|      |              |
|      |              |
|      |              |
|      |              |

Harcourt

Name _____

### Draw Conclusions

**1.** Where did the water travel? _____

_____

How do you know? _____

_____

**2.** How did the water travel? _____

_____

How do you know? _____

_____

**3.** **Scientists at Work** Scientists **infer** what happens in nature by making careful observations. Based on this investigation, what can you infer about the importance of stems? _____

_____

_____

**Investigate Further** How could you change a white carnation into a flower with two colors? Draw and write an explanation of your answer.

**My Explanation:** _____

_____

_____

Harcourt

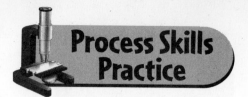

# Infer

Inferring is using what you observe to explain what has happened. An inference may be correct or incorrect. Once you have made an inference, you may need to make more observations to confirm your inference.

## Think About Inferring

Hope was helping decorate her house with flowers she cut from her garden. She made two similar bouquets in different vases with water. The pictures show what happened to Hope's bouquets after a few days. After the third day, Hope wondered why the flowers in the black vase stayed fresh, but those in the smaller white vase wilted. She looked inside the black vase. There was water in it. She looked inside the white vase. It was completely dry.

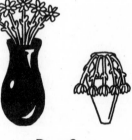

**Day 1**          **Day 2**          **Day 3**

**1.** What observations did Hope make? _____

_____

_____

_____

**2.** Infer why the flowers in the white vase wilted, but those in the black vase did

not. _____

_____

_____

**3.** What do you infer happened to the water in the white vase?

_____

_____

**4.** How could you test your inference? _____

_____

Harcourt

# How Are Plants Classified?

Plants are classified by whether or not they have tubes.

**Vocabulary**

| vascular plant (A18) | nonvascular plant (A20) |
|---|---|

**Fill in the blank with the letter of the correct answer.**

1. The main difference between plants and animals is that _____.
   **A** animals make their own food   **B** plants make their own food

2. In plants with tubes, the tubes _____.
   **A** take in air from around the plant
   **B** carry water, food, and nutrients to different plant parts

3. Where would you look for tubes in a plant? _____
   **A** in the stem   **B** in the leaves   **C** in the trunk   **D** all of these

4. In plants that do not have tubes, food travels in water _____.
   **A** around the outside of the plant   **B** from cell to cell

5. Nonvascular plants are always _____.
   **A** very small   **B** found in dry places

6. The _____ is the part of a tree trunk that has the living tubes.
   **A** heartwood   **B** sapwood

7. This tree was _____ when the trunk was cut down.
   **A** eight years old   **B** ten years old

8. Label the parts of the tree trunk.

   _____   _____

   _Growth ring_   _____

# Recognize Vocabulary

Match the definition in column A with the term in column B.

**Column A**

_____ 1. name of the second smallest group

_____ 2. animal with a backbone

_____ 3. plants with tubes

_____ 4. grouping things by a set of rules

_____ 5. name of the largest group

_____ 6. have many cells and absorb food from other living things

_____ 7. name of the smallest group

_____ 8. invertebrates with legs and several joints

_____ 9. plants without tubes

_____ 10. some one-celled with no nuclei

_____ 11. vertebrate that has fur and makes milk

_____ 12. invertebrates that may or may not have a hard shell

_____ 13. animal without a backbone

_____ 14. vertebrate that begins life in water

_____ 15. one-celled, no nuclei

_____ 16. vertebrate with dry, scaly skin

**Column B**

**A** mollusks

**B** fungi

**C** amphibian

**D** classification

**E** invertebrate

**F** nonvascular plants

**G** genus

**H** reptile

**I** kingdom

**J** mammal

**K** monerans

**L** species

**M** vascular plants

**N** protists

**O** arthropods

**P** vertebrate

# Chapter 2 • Graphic Organizer for Chapter Concepts

## Animal Growth and Adaptations

### LESSON 1
### BASIC NEEDS

Basic Needs
of Animals

1. _____

2. _____

3. _____

4. _____

5. _____

### LESSON 2
### BODY PARTS

Body Part Adaptations to
Meet Basic Needs

1. _____

2. _____

3. _____

4. _____

### LESSON 3
### BEHAVIORS

Behavior Adaptations to
Meet Basic Needs

1. _____

2. _____

3. _____

4. _____

Harcourt

# Basic Needs of Mealworms

## Materials

| | | | |
|---|---|---|---|
| plastic shoe box | bran meal | 3 shallow dishes | mealworms |
| flake cereal | 10-cm square of poster board | Spoon | water |

## Activity Procedure

1. Use the chart on the next page to **record** your observations and measurements.

2. **Measure** two spoonfuls of bran meal. Put them into a shallow dish. Put it at one end of the shoe box. Count 20 flakes of cereal. Put them into another shallow dish. Put this dish at the other end of the shoe box. Put a little water in the last shallow dish. Put it in the center of the shoe box.

3. Fold about 1 cm down on opposite sides of the poster board. It should stand up like a small table. Put it next to the water container.

4. Put the mealworms in the shoe box next to, but NOT in, the water. Put the lid on the box. Then put the shoe box in a dark place for an hour. Be careful not to spill anything.

5. Take the box to a dimly lit area. Open the lid, and **observe** the contents. Try to find the mealworms. **Record** your observations. Put the lid back on.

6. Put the box in a dark place overnight. Again, take the box to a dimly lit area. **Observe** the contents of the box. **Record** your observations. **Measure** the bran meal and count the cereal flakes. Record your measurements.

7. Put the box into bright sunshine for a few minutes. Does anything change? What can you **infer** from the location of the mealworms?

Harcourt

Name _____

| Mealworm Observations | | | | |
|---|---|---|---|---|
| Condition | Location | Size and Appearance | Food Measurements | Other |
| One hour in dark | | | | |
| Overnight in dark | | | | |
| Bright sunlight | | | | |

## Draw Conclusions

**1.** What happened to the mealworms? _____

_____

_____

_____

**2.** What happened to the food? _____

_____

_____

Why? _____

_____

**3. Scientists at Work** Scientists learn by **observing**. What can you **infer** about

animal needs by observing the mealworms? _____

_____

_____

_____

**Investigate Further** How could you find out which food the mealworms liked best? Plan an investigation. Decide what question you would like to answer and

what equipment you will need. _____

_____

_____

_____

Harcourt

Name _____

Date _____

# Observe and Infer

Observing is using your senses to notice details around you. An inference is a possible explanation of something you observed.

## Think About Observing and Inferring

Arthur enjoys watching the gray squirrels that scamper through his neighborhood. He decided to make a chart to record his observations of the squirrels. On his chart he also made inferences about how the squirrels were meeting their needs.

| Observations of Squirrels | Inferences About Needs |
|---|---|
| Squirrel runs up a tree close to the top and goes into leafy nest. | Squirrel uses the nest for shelter. |
| Squirrel opens a horse chestnut, takes a bite, and throws it away. | Squirrel is looking for good food to eat. |
| Squirrel jumps on birdbath and lowers its head near the water. | Squirrel is bathing its face and its paws. |
| Squirrel eats a sunflower seed under a birdfeeder. | Squirrel has found food it likes. |
| Squirrel carries a twig to the top of a tree and goes into its nest. | Squirrel wants to play a game with its babies. |

1. What inference might Arthur make about the squirrel's diet?

   _____

   _____

   _____

2. Evaluate Arthur's other inferences. Which observations would you consider

   good evidence for or against each of these inferences? _____

   _____

   _____

   _____

   _____

Harcourt

# What Are The Basic Needs of Animals?

## Lesson Concept

All animals have common basic needs.

## Vocabulary

**environment** (A32)  **climate** (A33)  **oxygen** (A33)

**shelter** (A35)  **metamorphosis** (A36)

**Fill in the blank with the correct vocabulary term. Use the words in the list above.**

**1.** Everything that surrounds and affects a living thing is called its

_____.

**2.** Some insects molt, form a chrysalis around their bodies, and change from larvae to adults. This process of changing body shape is called

_____.

**List the needs all animals have by filling in the diagram below. For each of the needs, write an example of how one animal fulfills that need. The first one has been done as an example.**

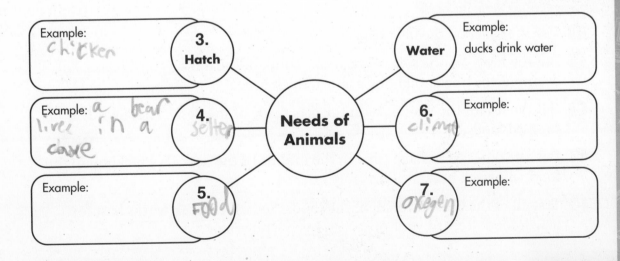

Name _____

Date _____

# Bird Beaks and Food

## Materials

| | | | |
|---|---|---|---|
| cooked rice | raisins | plastic worms | paper plates |
| birdseed | cooked spaghetti | forceps | |
| peanuts in shells | chopsticks or blunt pencils | water in a cup | |
| spoon | pliers | clothespin | |

## Activity Procedure

1. Use the chart on the next page.

2. Put the tools on one side of the desk. Think of the tools as bird beaks. For example, the pliers might be a short, thick beak.

3. Put the rest of the materials on the other side of the desk. They stand for bird foods.

4. Put one type of food at a time in the middle of the desk. Try picking up the food with each beak.

5. **Test** all of the beaks with all of the foods. See which beak works best for which food. **Record** your observations in your chart.

Harcourt

**Investigate Log**

| Bird-Food and Beak Observations | | |
|---|---|---|
| **Food** | **Best Tool (Beak)** | **Observations** |
| plastic worms | | |
| cooked spaghetti | | |
| cooked rice | | |
| raisins | | |
| birdseed | | |
| peanuts in shells | | |
| water | | |

## Draw Conclusions

1. Which kind of beak is best for picking up each food? _____

_____

_____

_____

Which is best for crushing seeds? _____

_____

2. By **observing** the shape of a bird's beak, what can you **infer** about the food the

bird eats? _____

_____

3. **Scientists at Work** Scientists often **use models** to help them test ideas. How

did using models help you test ideas about bird beaks? _____

_____

_____

**Investigate Further** Find a book about birds. Identify real birds that have beaks like the tools you used in this investigation. Make a booklet describing each beak type and how birds use it to gather and eat food. Include your own pictures of the beaks and of the matching foods each beak can best gather and eat.

Name _____

Date _____

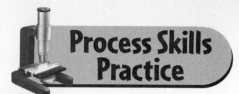

# Make and Use Models

Books have pictures of different animals with unusual adaptations. You can make and use models of these adaptations to learn more about how they help animals meet their needs.

## Think About Making and Using Models

Malcolm read in a book that the toucan's beak was large but very light. Malcolm wondered how the bird used its large beak. He decided to make a model of the toucan's beak. He cut a wide cardboard tube in half lengthwise and hinged the two halves together with paper fasteners. He made cuts in the ends of the tube to make a curved point. He cut jagged edges in the model to look like a toucan's beak.

Malcolm used his model to try to pick up the foods listed on the chart. The chart shows his results.

| Food | How Toucan Beak Model Performed |
|------|-------------------------------|
| Plastic insects | OK; hard to grab with tip because hard |
| Plastic worms | OK; easier to grab because soft |
| Blueberries | Good; easy to grab because soft and larger than raisins |
| Whole peach | Very good; easy to grab because soft and large |
| Peanuts in shell | OK; hard to grab because hard |
| Birdseed | Poor; seeds too small to pick up with beak |

1. What conclusions could Malcolm draw from his results? _____

   _____

   _____

2. How was Malcolm's model like a real toucan beak? _____

   _____

   How was it different? _____

   _____

   _____

4. How could Malcolm evaluate whether or not his model gave him good results?

   _____

Harcourt

Use with page A39.

Name _____

Date _____

# How Do Animals' Body Parts Help Them Meet Their Needs?

## Lesson Concept

Animals have adaptations, which enable them to meet their needs.

## Vocabulary

| **adaptation** (A40) | **camouflage** (A44) | **mimicry** (A44) |
| --- | --- | --- |

The ptarmigan (TAR•mih•guhn) is a white bird that lives in the harsh environment near the tops of mountains and also in the Arctic. It eats leaves and mosses and lichens that grow on rocks. Study the picture of the ptarmigan, and write about how each of the body parts listed below is an adaptation that helps the ptarmigan meet its needs. Use at least one of the vocabulary terms.

Feathers _____

_____

Color _____

_____

Feet _____

_____

Bones _____

_____

Beak _____

_____

Name _____

Date _____

# Monarch Butterfly Travel

## Materials

outline map of
North America

2 pencils of
different colors

## Activity Procedure

1. Label the directions north, south, east, and west on your map.

2. During the summer many monarch butterflies live in two general areas. Some live in the northeastern United States and around the shores of the Great Lakes. Others live along the southwestern coast of Canada and in the states of Washington and Oregon. Locate these two large general areas on your map. Shade each area a different color.

3. At summer's end large groups of monarchs gather and travel south for the winter. Most of those east of the Rocky Mountains fly to the mountains of central Mexico. But some of these butterflies make their way to Florida. Butterflies west of the Rocky Mountains fly to sites along the California coast. All of these areas have trees where the butterflies can rest, temperatures that are cool yet above freezing, and water to drink. Find these areas on your map. Shade each winter area the same color as the matching summer area. Then use the right color to draw the most direct route from north to south over land.

Harcourt

Name _____

## Draw Conclusions

**1. Compare** the climate where the monarch butterflies spend the summer with the climate where they spend the winter. _____

_____

_____

**2.** What can you **infer** about how the behavior of the butterflies helps them meet their needs? _____

_____

_____

**3. Scientists at Work** Scientists use maps and graphs to **communicate** data and ideas visually. How does making a map of butterfly movements help you understand where monarchs travel? _____

_____

_____

_____

**Investigate Further** Many kinds of birds, fish, and mammals travel to different places when the seasons change. Research the travel route of one of these animals. Use a map to show the route.

**My animal:** _____

**Where it travels:** _____

_____

**Why it travels:** _____

_____

Harcourt

Name _____

Date _____

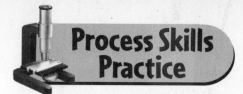

# Communicate

When you communicate, you give information to someone. You can use words or a map or both to communicate information about animal migration.

## Think About Communicating

Read the information about the migration routes and schedules of some North American birds. Use pencils of different colors to trace the path that each type of bird follows on its migration.

   The common tern winters along the coast of southern Florida. It flies north, reaching the southern edge of the Great Lakes by May 1. It reaches its summer range in central-western Canada by June 1.

   The short-eared owl winters everywhere in the United States. Some owls migrate north into Canada for the summer. They reach central Canada by May 1. Those that fly all the way to the Arctic arrive by June 1.

   The ruby-throated hummingbird winters in central Mexico. These birds all migrate to the eastern half of the United States for the summer. Some stay in the south. Others continue migrating north. Those that migrate north reach the Smoky Mountains by April 1 and an area just south of the Great Lakes by May 1.

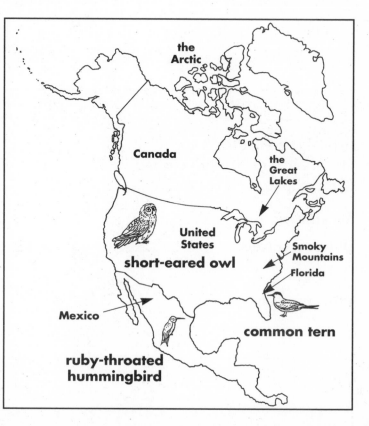

Of the two forms of communication used here, the words and the map, which

gave you the most information the most quickly? Explain. _____

_____

_____

_____

Harcourt

Name _____

Date _____

 **Concept Review**

# How Do Animals' Behaviors Help Them Meet Their Needs?

## Lesson Concept

Animals behave in ways that enable them to meet their needs. The behaviors are adaptations to their environments.

## Vocabulary

| instinct (A48) | migration (A49) | hibernation (A51) |
|---|---|---|

1. For each behavior, write **I** if it is an instinct or **L** if it is a learned behavior.

    _I_ Atlantic green turtles migrate to Ascension Island.

    _I_ Ground squirrels hibernate during the winter.

    _L_ Mother tigers hunt for food.

    _L_ You read this worksheet.

    _I_ Pacific salmon return to the stream where they hatched.

    _L_ Chimpanzees call to one another.

2. How could a scientist determine if a behavior is an instinct or is learned?

    _By doing an observation and_
    _an experiment._

3. Many places are very cold during the winter. If an animal does not have adaptations to live through the cold winter, what two things could it do to survive until the spring? What must the animal have to do these things?

    _Hibernat and migrat_

Harcourt

Name _____

Date _____

# Recognize Vocabulary

Use the terms below to fill in the word puzzle.

| | | | |
|---|---|---|---|
| environment | climate | oxygen | shelter |
| metamorphosis | adaptation | camouflage | mimicry |
| instinct | migration | hibernation | |

**Across**

3. helps an animal blend with its surroundings

5. a behavior an animal is born with

7. changes made from an egg to a larva to an adult

9. the movement from one region to another and back again

10. a body part or behavior that helps an animal meet its needs

**Down**

1. everything that surrounds and affects an animal

2. a long, deep "sleep"

3. average temperature and rainfall

4. an animal looks much like another animal or object

6. a place where an animal can protect itself

8. a gas in the air animals need

Harcourt

# Chapter 3 • Graphic Organizer for Chapter Concepts

## Plant Growth and Adaptations

### LESSON 1
### BASIC NEEDS OF PLANTS

Needs

1. _____

2. _____

3. _____

4. _____

### LESSON 2
### BASIC PLANT PARTS

Parts

1. _____

2. _____

3. _____

### LESSON 3
### WAYS PLANTS REPRODUCE

Way        Example

1. _____

2. _____

3. _____

4. _____

5. _____

6. _____

Harcourt

# How Light Affects Plants

## Materials

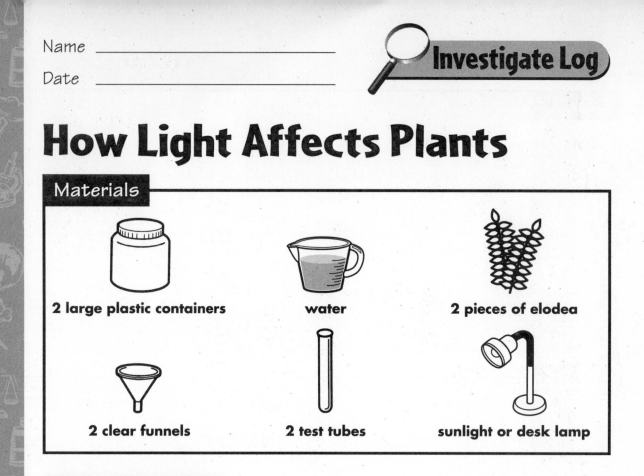

2 large plastic containers     water     2 pieces of elodea

2 clear funnels     2 test tubes     sunlight or desk lamp

## Activity Procedure

1. Fill one container about $\frac{2}{3}$ full of water. Place one piece of elodea in the water.

2. Turn a funnel wide side down, and place it in the water over the elodea. There should be enough water in the container so that the small end of the funnel is just below the water.

3. Fill a test tube with water. Cover the end with your thumb and turn the tube upside down. Place the test tube over the end of the funnel. Allow as little water as possible to escape from the tube.

4. Repeat Steps 1–3 using the second container, funnel, piece of elodea, and test tube.

5. Set one container of elodea in sunlight or under a desk lamp. Set the other in a dark place, such as a closet.

6. After several hours, **observe** the contents of each container.

Harcourt

Name _____

## Draw Conclusions

1. **Compare** the two test tubes. What do you **observe?** _____

_____

_____

2. One test tube is now partly filled with a gas. What can you **infer** about where the gas came from? _____

_____

_____

3. **Scientists at Work** Scientists **control variables** to learn what effect each condition has on the outcome of an experiment. What one variable did you change in this investigation? _____

_____

What variables were the same in both containers? _____

_____

_____

**Investigate Further** How fast can a plant make oxygen? Repeat the procedure for the plant placed in light, but use a graduate instead of a test tube. **Measure** the amount of air in the graduate every 15 minutes for 2 hours. **Record** your findings. Make a line graph to show how fast the plant produced oxygen.

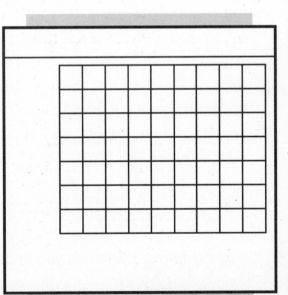

Harcourt

Name _____

Date _____

# Identify and Control Variables

Identifying and controlling variables helps you set up an investigation. These results may show you what you want to find out. For your investigation to work, you need to change one variable related to what you want to know. You keep all the other variables the same.

## Think About Identifying and Controlling Variables

Raphael read that plants get nutrients from the soil. He wanted to check this information by doing an experiment. He took two plants of the same type and size and planted one in a pot containing small plastic plant pellets and the other in a pot containing the same amount of potting soil. He put the plants next to each other in a sunny window and watered them with equal amounts of water every three days. Every week he observed the plants closely, measured their growth, and recorded his observations. The picture shows a page from Raphael's observation journal after the second month of the experiment.

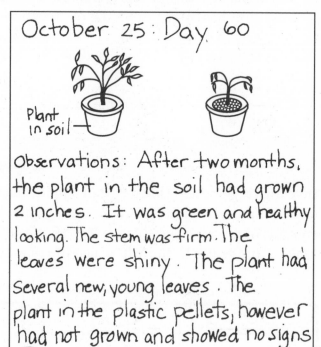

October 25: Day 60

Plant in soil

Observations: After two months, the plant in the soil had grown 2 inches. It was green and healthy looking. The stem was firm. The leaves were shiny. The plant had several new, young leaves. The plant in the plastic pellets, however, had not grown and showed no signs

**1.** Which variables did Raphael control in this experiment?

_____

_____

**2.** What did Raphael vary and why? _____

_____

**3.** Compare the two plants. Do you think Raphael's results gave evidence that

plants get nutrients from the soil? Explain. _____

_____

Harcourt

**Use with page A63.**

Name _____

Date _____

# What Do Plants Need to Live?

## Lesson Concept

Plants have adaptations to help them meet their needs.

## Vocabulary

**carbon dioxide** (A64)    **nutrient** (A64)    **photosynthesis** (A65)

**Answer the questions below about plants.**

**1.** List the basic needs of plants by filling in the diagram below. For each need, tell how the substance is used. Use vocabulary terms when possible.

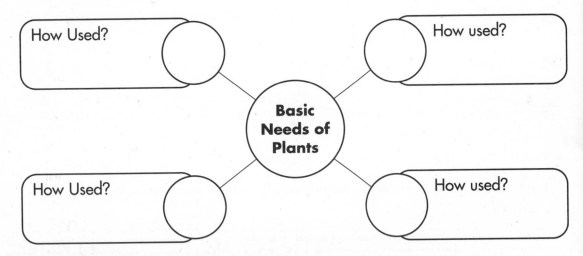

**For each of the plants listed below, describe one adaptation it has and tell how the adaptation helps the plant.**

**2.** Vine _____

_____

**3.** Cactus _____

_____

**4.** Water lily _____

_____

_____

Name _____

Date _____

# How Plants "Breathe"

## Materials

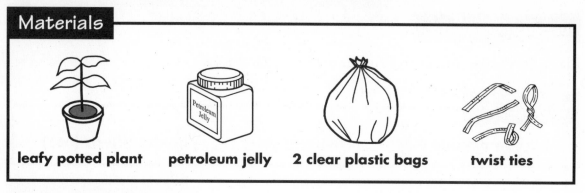

leafy potted plant     petroleum jelly     2 clear plastic bags     twist ties

## Activity Procedure

1. Use the chart below.

2. Put a thin layer of petroleum jelly on both the top and bottom surfaces of a leaf on the plant.

3. Put a plastic bag over the leaf. Gently tie the bag closed. Do this just below the place where the leaf attaches to the stem.

4. Put a plastic bag over a second leaf and seal it. Do not put any petroleum jelly on this leaf.

5. Put the plant in a place that gets plenty of light, and water it normally.

6. After two days, **observe** the two leaves. **Record** your observations on your chart.

| Plant Leaf | Observations |
|---|---|
| Leaf with petroleum jelly | |
| Leaf with no petroleum jelly | |

Harcourt

Name _____

## Draw Conclusions

1. **Compare** the two plastic bags. What do you **observe?** _____

_____

_____

_____

2. What can you **infer** from what you **observed** in this investigation?

_____

_____

_____

_____

_____

3. **Scientists at Work** Scientists often **compare** objects or events. Comparing allows the scientists to see the effects of the variables they control. Compare the leaves you used in this investigation. What can you **infer** about the effect of the

petroleum jelly? _____

_____

_____

**Investigate Further** Find out where gases are exchanged in a leaf. This time, coat the top side of one leaf and the bottom side of another leaf. Tie a plastic bag over

each leaf. What do you **observe? My observations:** _____

_____

What can you **infer?** _____

_____

_____

Harcourt

Name _____

Date _____

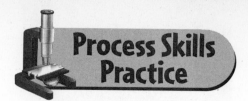

# Compare

When you compare objects or events, you look for what they have in common. You also look for differences between them.

## Think About Comparing

Atea knows that dandelions and irises are flowers. But they look different. She finds pictures of both these flowers. She compares them to see what is the same and what is different.

1. How are the roots of these two plants different? _____

_____

_____

2. How are the leaves of these two plants different? _____

_____

_____

3. How do you think the roots and leaves of these plants are alike? Consider what they do for the plant. _____

_____

_____

_____

4. How are the stems of the two plants alike? How are they different?

_____

_____

Harcourt

Name _____

Date _____

**Concept Review**

# How Do Leaves, Stems, and Roots Help Plants Live?

## Lesson Concept

Plants have leaf, stem, and root adaptations that help them meet their needs. Some plants have parts that trap and digest insects to get needed nutrients.

## Vocabulary

**symmetry** (A70)   **transpiration** (A70)   **taproot** (A71)   **fibrous root** (A71)

**Write the letter of the best answer to each question on the line.**

1. The two main leaf types are

   _____.

   **A** broad leaves and needle leaves
   **B** flat leaves and needle leaves
   **C** broad leaves and spines

2. The main functions of most leaves

   are to _____.
   **A** take in moisture and give off gases
   **B** take in moisture and give support
   **C** carry on photosynthesis and exchange gases

3. The main functions of most stems

   are to _____.
   **A** carry on photosynthesis
   **B** support plants and give them shape
   **C** protect plants and store food

4. Compared with fibrous roots, a

   taproot is _____.
   **A** thin and grows near the surface of the soil
   **B** thick and grows deep into the soil
   **C** has long, branching root hairs growing from it

5. Meat-eating plants trap insects,

   because _____.
   **A** they cannot make their own food
   **B** they cannot absorb enough sunlight
   **C** their soil lacks enough nutrients

6. Transpiration occurs in a plant when

   _____.
   **A** the leaves trap an insect
   **B** the leaves give off water
   **C** the roots give off water

# Seedling Growth

## Materials

2 paper towels    small, clear jar or cup    water    alfalfa seed

bean seed    hand lens    yarn    ruler

## Activity Procedure

1. Fold the paper towel, and place it around the inside of the jar.

2. Make a second paper towel into a ball, and place it inside the jar to fill the space.

3. Place the alfalfa seed about 3 cm from the top of the jar, between the paper-towel lining and the jar's side. You should be able to see the seed through the jar.

4. Place the bean seed in a similar position on the other side of the jar.

5. Pour water into the jar to soak the towels completely.

6. Set the jar in a sunny place, and leave it there for five days. Be sure to keep the paper towels moist.

7. Use the chart on the next page.

8. Use the hand lens to **observe** the seeds daily for five days. **Measure** the growth of the roots and shoots with the yarn. Use the ruler to measure the yarn. **Record** your observations on your chart.

Harcourt

Name _____

| Seed Growth | | | | |
|---|---|---|---|---|
| | Alfalfa | | Bean | |
| | Size | Other Observations | Size | Other Observations |
| Day 1 | | | | |
| Day 2 | | | | |
| Day 3 | | | | |
| Day 4 | | | | |
| Day 5 | | | | |

## Draw Conclusions

1. What plant parts grew from each seed? _____
_____

2. **Compare** the growth of the roots and the shoots from the two seeds. Did they grow to be the same size? _____
_____
_____

Did they grow at the same rate? _____
_____
_____

3. **Scientists at Work** Scientists take a lot of care to **measure** objects the same way each time. Think about how you measured the plants. How do you know your measurements were accurate? _____
_____
_____

**Investigate Further** The bean and alfalfa seedlings will continue to grow after the first five days. Plant each of the seedlings in soil. Give the seedlings the same amount of water and light. Continue **observing** and **recording** information about your plants for a month. Make a drawing of your plants each week. Identify and label the parts of the plants.

Harcourt

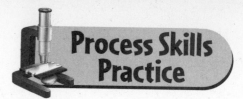

# Measure

Measuring is a way to observe and compare objects and events accurately. When you measure, you may want to use an instrument, such as a ruler, a balance, or a stopwatch.

## Think About Measuring

A group of students wanted to find out how much food three different kinds of corn plants would produce. They formed two teams. Each team grew ten plants of each kind of corn. When the plants were grown, they harvested the corn. To figure out how much food each type of corn produced, both teams removed all the ears of corn from the stalks. They removed the husks from around the corn. Team 1 cut the corn kernels from the cob and used a balance to find the mass of the corn kernels. Team 2 measured the mass of whole ears of corn. The following table shows both teams' results.

| Corn Produced | | | |
|------|--------|--------|--------|
| Team | Corn A | Corn B | Corn C |
| 1 | 5 kg | 2.5 kg | 2 kg |
| 2 | 10 kg | 8 kg | 6.5 kg |

1. Could the teams get the answer to their question about which types of corn produced the most food based on their results? Explain your answer.

   _____

   _____

2. Whose method of measuring how much food each kind of corn plant produced was most accurate, Team 1's or Team 2's? Explain your answer.

   _____

   _____

3. If the students had just counted the number of ears produced by each plant type, would they come to the same conclusions?

   _____

   _____

# How Do Plants Reproduce?

## Lesson Concept

Plants reproduce in many ways.

## Vocabulary

| germinate (A76) | spore (A77) | tuber (A79) |
|---|---|---|

**Tell how the seed in each picture would be most likely to spread.**

1. _____

_____

_____

_____

2. _____

_____

_____

_____

3. How are spores different from seeds? _____

_____

_____

_____

4. Describe four ways people can grow new plants without planting seeds.

_____

_____

_____

_____

_____

_____

Harcourt

# Recognize Vocabulary

Read the following sentences. On each line, write the letter for the word or words that best go with the underlined words.

| carbon dioxide | nutrient | photosynthesis | symmetry |
| transpiration | taproot | fibrous root | germinate |
| spore | tuber | | |

_____ 1. To make food, plants need <u>gas breathed out by animals</u>.

     **A** carbon dioxide    **B** nutrients    **C** spore

_____ 2. Trapping sunlight to make food energy is <u>the process that makes food in a plant</u>.

     **A** transpiration    **B** germination    **C** photosynthesis

_____ 3. Grass is a plant that has <u>many roots of the same size</u>.

     **A** taproots    **B** tubers    **C** fibrous roots

_____ 4. A seed <u>sprouts</u> when its need for water, air, and warmth is met.

     **A** tubers    **B** germinates    **C** spores

_____ 5. Plants can lose water through <u>the process in which water is given off by plant parts</u>.

     **A** transpiration    **B** symmetry    **C** photosynthesis

_____ 6. Leaves have <u>two halves that look like mirror images</u>.

     **A** spores    **B** symmetry    **C** transpiration

_____ 7. Soil provides plants with <u>substances needed for growth</u>.

     **A** carbon dioxide    **B** nutrients    **C** spores

_____ 8. Some plants form <u>tiny cells</u> to make new plants.

     **A** tubers    **B** nutrients    **C** spores

_____ 9. <u>Swollen underground stems</u> can be used to make new plants.

     **A** tubers    **B** nutrients    **C** spores

_____ 10. Dandelions have <u>one main root that goes deep into the soil</u>.

     **A** fibrous roots    **B** tubers    **C** taproots

Harcourt

# Chapter 4 • Graphic Organizer for Chapter Concepts

## Body Systems

### LESSON 1
### SKELETAL SYSTEM

What It Does

_____

_____

_____

Main Parts

1. _____

2. _____

### LESSON 2
### RESPIRATORY SYSTEM

What It Does

_____

_____

Main Part

1. _____

### LESSON 3
### NERVOUS SYSTEM

What It Does

_____

_____

_____

Main Parts

1. _____

2. _____

3. _____

4. _____

### MUSCULAR SYSTEM

What It Does

_____

_____

Main Parts

1. _____

2. _____

3. _____

### CIRCULATORY SYSTEM

What It Does

_____

_____

Main Parts

1. _____

2. _____

3. _____

4. _____

### DIGESTIVE SYSTEM

What It Does

_____

_____

_____

Main Parts

1. _____

2. _____

3. _____

4. _____

Name _____

Date _____

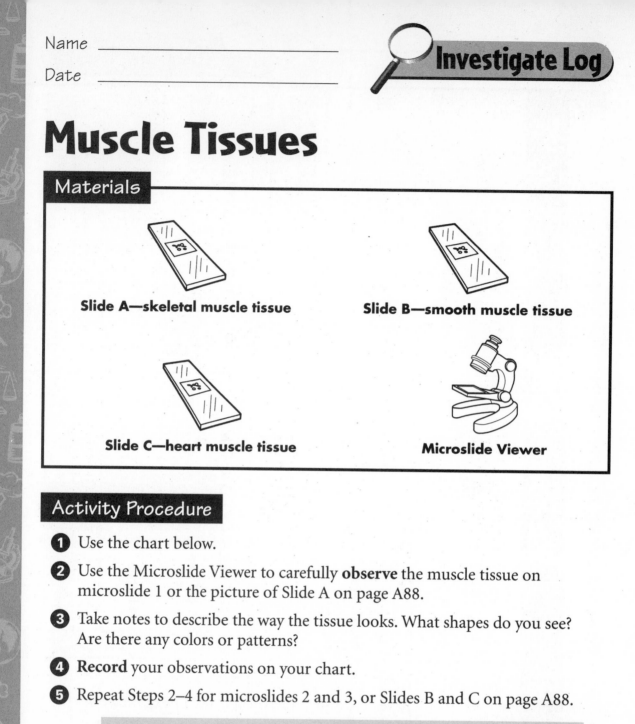

# Investigate Log

# Muscle Tissues

## Materials

Slide A—skeletal muscle tissue

Slide B—smooth muscle tissue

Slide C—heart muscle tissue

Microslide Viewer

## Activity Procedure

1. Use the chart below.

2. Use the Microslide Viewer to carefully **observe** the muscle tissue on microslide 1 or the picture of Slide A on page A88.

3. Take notes to describe the way the tissue looks. What shapes do you see? Are there any colors or patterns?

4. **Record** your observations on your chart.

5. Repeat Steps 2–4 for microslides 2 and 3, or Slides B and C on page A88.

| Type of Muscle | Observations | Ways Like Other Types of Muscle | Ways Different from Other Types of Muscles |
|---|---|---|---|
| Slide A | | | |
| Slide B | | | |
| Slide C | | | |

(page 1 of 2)

Harcourt

**Investigate Log**

## Draw Conclusions

1. Describe each type of muscle tissue.

   Slide A _____

   _____

   Slide B _____

   _____

   Slide C _____

   _____

2. How do the tissues look the same? _____

   _____

   How do they look different? _____

   _____

   _____

   _____

3. **Scientists at Work** Many scientists use microscopes in their work. What does a microscope do that makes it possible to **observe** and **compare** muscle tissues?

   _____

   _____

   _____

   _____

**Investigate Further** If you have access to a microscope, use one to **observe** prepared slides of different kinds of tissue. See page R4 for help in using a microscope. Cells from different kinds of tissue in your body look different. Find pictures of other kinds of tissue, such as nerve tissue, bone tissue, and blood tissue. **Compare** these tissues with the muscle tissues you looked at.

Harcourt

Name _____

Date _____

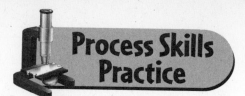

**Process Skills Practice**

# Observe and Compare

Looking at something closely is one way of observing. You extend your sense of sight when you use a hand lens or a microscope. As you make observations, you may compare the different things you observe.

## Think About Comparing

Your blood is made up of a variety of different cells floating in a watery fluid. Study the diagrams of different types of blood cells, as they would appear stained and under a microscope. Then answer the questions.

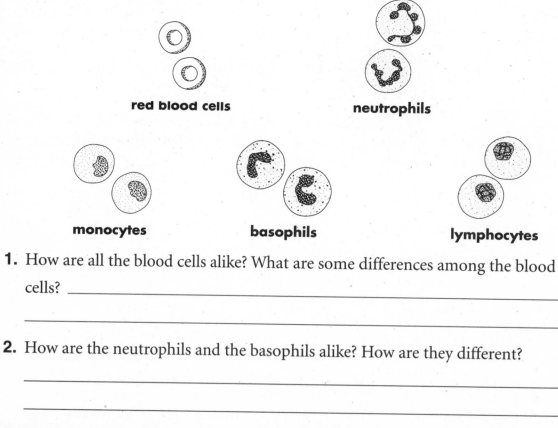

red blood cells          neutrophils

monocytes          basophils          lymphocytes

1. How are all the blood cells alike? What are some differences among the blood cells? _____

   _____

2. How are the neutrophils and the basophils alike? How are they different?

   _____

   _____

3. How are the monocytes and the lymphocytes alike? _____

   _____

4. How do the neutrophil and basophil both differ from the monocyte and lymphocyte? How do all four of these cells differ from red blood cells?

   _____

   _____

Harcourt

Name _____

Date _____

# How Do the Skeletal and Muscular Systems Work?

## Lesson Concept

The skeletal and muscular systems work together to help the body move.

### Vocabulary

| | | |
|---|---|---|
| **cell** (A90) | **tissue** (A90) | **organ** (A90) |
| **cardiac muscle** (A91) | **smooth muscle** (A91) | **striated muscle** (A92) |

Fill in the diagram to describe the basic parts that make up your body.

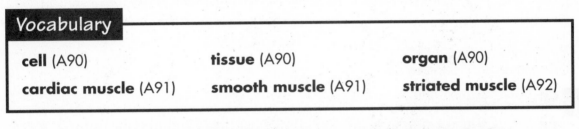

cells → form → 1. tissue → form → 2. organ → form → a system

example ↓     example ↓     example ↓     example ↓

3. bone cells

4. bone tissue

5. bones

6. skeletal system

List four functions of your skeletal system.

7. support your body     help you move
give body shape     protect the organs

Identify each type of muscle tissue, and tell where it is in the body.

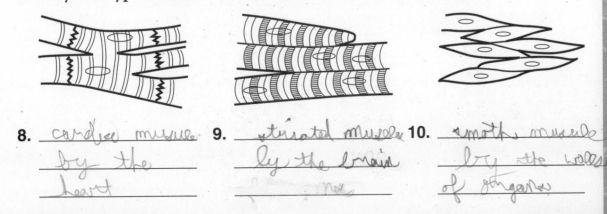

8. cardiac muscle by the heart

9. striated muscle by the brain

10. smooth muscle by the walls of organs

Harcourt

# Breathing Rates

## Materials

**stopwatch, timer, or clock with second hand**

## Activity Procedure

1. Use the chart below.

2. While you are sitting, count the number of times you breathe out in one minute. **Record** the number on your chart.

3. Stand up and march in place for one minute. Raise your knees as high as you can. As soon as you stop marching, begin to count the number of times you breathe out. Count your breaths for one minute. **Record** the number of breaths on your chart.

4. Rest for a few minutes, and then run in place for one minute. As soon as you stop running, begin to count the number of times you breathe out. Count your breaths for one minute. **Record** the number on your chart.

5. Make a bar graph to show how your breathing changed for each activity.

| Activity | Number of Breaths |
|---|---|
| Sitting | |
| After marching for 1 minute | |
| After running for 1 minute | |

Harcourt

## Draw Conclusions

1. Which activity needed the fewest breaths? _____

   Which needed the most breaths? _____

2. What can you **infer** about breathing from what happened in this investigation?

   _____

   _____

   _____

3. **Scientists at Work**  Scientists don't usually **measure** something just once. What could you do to be sure your breathing rate measurements were correct?

   _____

   _____

   _____

**Investigate Further**  Does your breathing rate increase if you exercise longer? March in place for two minutes, and then count your breaths. Run in place for two minutes, and then count your breaths. Add two new rows to your chart, and **record** the numbers.

| Activity | Number of Breaths |
|---|---|
| Sitting | |
| After marching for 1 minute | |
| After running for 1 minute | |
| After marching for 2 minutes | |
| After running for 2 minutes | |

Harcourt

Name _____

Date _____

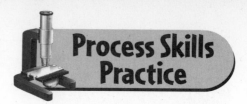

# Measure

When you make observations that involve numbers, usually you are measuring. You can use an instrument, such as a ruler, a stopwatch, or the device shown below, to make measurements.

## Think About Measuring

Taylor was interested in finding out how much air people can hold in their lungs. She looked in a science book and found instructions for making a device that measures how much air people can breathe out. She made the device, called a spirometer (spy•RAH•MUH•ter) as shown. She used the device to measure how much air her classmates could breathe out in one breath. Her results are listed on the chart. (Air volume is measured in cubic centimeters.)

| Subject | Amount of Air Breathed Out |
|---------|---------------------------|
| Melissa | 1400 cc |
| Jordan | 1500 cc |
| Sam | 1700 cc |
| Charlotte | 1500 cc |
| Latasha | 1400 cc |
| Paul | 600 cc |
| Ricardo | 1200 cc |
| Patricia | 1300 cc |
| Rita | 1400 cc |
| Robbie | 1600 cc |
| Ms. Bell | 2100 cc |

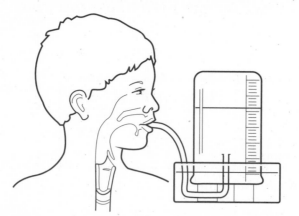

**1.** What was Taylor measuring and how did she make her measurements?

_____

**2.** Taylor thought that some of her measurements might be wrong. Which measurements do you think she might be worried about? Why?

_____

_____

**3.** What do you think Taylor should do about the possible faulty measurements?

_____

_____

Harcourt

**Use with page A95.**

# How Do the Respiratory and Circulatory Systems Work?

## Lesson Concept

The respiratory and circulatory systems deliver oxygen to the body and remove wastes.

## Vocabulary

**lungs** (A96)     **capillary** (A96)     **heart** (A97)     **artery** (A97)     **vein** (A97)

**Answer the questions below.**

1. What happens in the lung's air sacs, shown at the right?

   _____

   _____

   _____

   _____

   _____

2. List in order the types of blood vessels blood travels through as it goes from the heart to the body cells and back again. What happens in the blood vessels

   near the body cells? _____

   _____

   _____

3. How do your heart and lungs work together to carry out their main functions?

   _____

   _____

   _____

   _____

   _____

   _____

Harcourt

# The Sense of Touch

## Materials

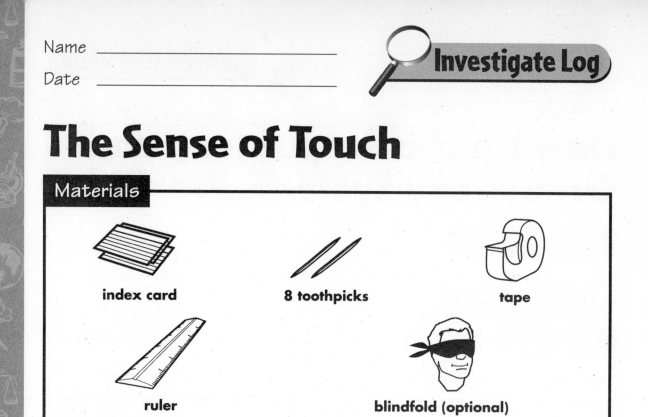

index card

8 toothpicks

tape

ruler

blindfold (optional)

## Activity Procedure

1. Use the chart on the next page.

2. Look at the areas of the body listed on the chart. **Predict** which one has the best sense of touch. Write your prediction on the chart. Explain your choice.

3. Measure a space 1 cm wide on one edge of the index card. Mark each end of the space, and write the distance between the marks. Tape a toothpick to each mark so that one end of each toothpick sticks out about 1 cm past the edge of the card. Make sure the toothpicks point straight out from the edge of the card.

4. Repeat Step 3 for the other three sides of the index card. However, use spaces 2 cm, 5 cm, and 8 cm wide, one for each side.

5. Have a partner test your sense of touch. Ask him or her to lightly touch one body area listed on the chart with the toothpicks on each edge of the index card. Begin with the 1-cm side, then use each side in turn with spaces 2 cm apart, 5 cm apart, and 8 cm apart. Don't watch as your partner does this.

6. For each area, tell your partner when you first feel two separate toothpicks touching your skin. Have your partner write the distance between these toothpicks on the chart.

7. Switch roles and test your partner.

Harcourt

Name _____

| Distance Between Toothpicks When Two Toothpicks First Felt | | |
|---|---|---|
| | **Palm** | **Lower Arm** | **Upper Arm** |
| Prediction | | | |
| Actual | | | |

## Draw Conclusions

**1.** Which of the body parts felt the two toothpicks the shortest distance apart?

_____

**2.** Based on this test, which of these body parts would you **infer** has the best sense of touch? Explain. _____

_____

**3. Scientists at Work** Using what you observed in this investigation, which part of your body do you **predict** to be more sensitive, your fingertip or the back of your neck? _____

**Investigate Further** Have your partner use the toothpicks to test your fingertip and the back of your neck to check the **prediction** you just made.

**My observations:** _____

_____

_____

_____

Name _____

Date _____

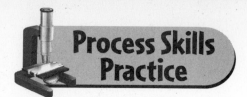

# Predict

Predicting involves telling what you think will happen in the future. You make predictions based on observations you have made before or experiences you have had in the past.

## Think About Predicting

Mr. Brown's class was learning about how the nervous system works. They learned that with practice, they could increase how fast they could send messages from their brains to their muscles. This is called improving reaction time.

The class decided to do an experiment to see if practicing to music could help them improve their reaction time even more than practice without music would. The class formed one large circle, with all

| Reaction Time: | | |
|---|---|---|
| **No Music** | **Slow Music** | **Fast Music** |
| 28 seconds | 28 seconds | 27 seconds |
| 27 seconds | 26 seconds | 24 seconds |
| 25 seconds | 24 seconds | 24 seconds |
| 24 seconds | 24 seconds | 25 seconds |
| 22 seconds | 22 seconds | 21 seconds |
| 23 seconds | 22 seconds | 19 seconds |
| 22 seconds | 23 seconds | 17 seconds |
| 21 seconds | 22 seconds | 16 seconds |

the students holding hands. Two students near the teacher broke hands, so that these students were holding the hand of only one other student. Mr. Brown gave one of these students a stopwatch. When Mr. Brown said, "Go," the student with the stopwatch started it running; the other student squeezed the hand of the student next to him or her. As soon as that student felt the squeeze, he or she would squeeze the hand of the next student. When the student holding the stopwatch felt the squeeze, he or she stopped the timer and announced the class reaction time. The class did the next trial with slow music and the third trial with fast music. They did eight of each kind of trial in sequence, as described.

1. Based on these results, how could the class improve their reaction time even more? On what observations or experience do you base this prediction?

_____

_____

_____

_____

_____

# How Do the Nervous and Digestive Systems Work?

## Lesson Concept

The brain controls the way all other body systems work. The digestive system breaks down food to provide nutrients for all the body's cells.

## Vocabulary

**brain** (A102)          **neuron** (A102)          **nerve** (A102)

**spinal cord** (A102)    **esophagus** (A104)       **stomach** (A104)

**small intestine** (A104)    **large intestine** (A105)

**Answer the questions below.**

**1.** What does your nervous system do? _____

_____

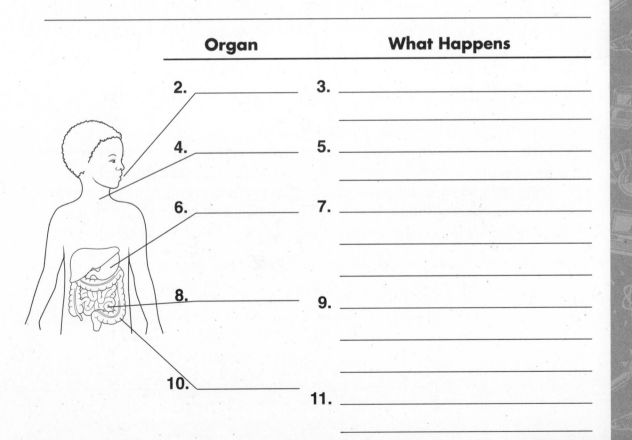

| Organ | What Happens |
|---|---|
| 2. | 3. |
| 4. | 5. |
| 6. | 7. |
| 8. | 9. |
| 10. | 11. |

Harcourt

Name _____

Date _____

# Recognize Vocabulary

In the space provided, write the letter of the term in Column B that best fits the definition in Column A.

### Column A

_____ 1. This blood vessel carries blood away from the heart.

_____ 2. This muscle makes up the heart.

_____ 3. The basic building block of the body

_____ 4. Connects nerves in your body to your brain

_____ 5. Type of muscle found in the walls of your organs

_____ 6. This blood vessel carries blood to the heart.

_____ 7. The control center of your nervous system

_____ 8. This kind of blood vessel is the smallest.

_____ 9. This is formed from tissues of different kinds working together.

_____ 10. These organs take oxygen into your body.

_____ 11. This kind of tissue makes up the muscles in your arms and legs.

_____ 12. This organ pumps blood throughout your body.

_____ 13. Water is removed from digested food here.

_____ 14. Food is liquified in this organ.

_____ 15. Food is digested the most here and taken into the body.

_____ 16. These connect the sense organs in your head to your brain.

_____ 17. Cells of the same type form this.

_____ 18. These cells are the basic unit of the nervous system.

_____ 19. Tube that goes from your mouth to your stomach

### Column B

A  vein

B  brain

C  organ

D  cardiac muscle

E  spinal cord

F  esophagus

G  nerves

H  stomach

I  small intestine

J  neurons

K  large intestine

L  tissue

M  smooth muscle

N  cell

O  capillary

P  striated muscle

Q  lungs

R  heart

S  artery

Use with pages A88–A105.

# Chapter 1 • Graphic Organizer for Chapter Concepts

## Ecosystems

### LESSON 1
### SYSTEMS

Definition _____

Types of Systems

1. _____
2. _____

Examples of Systems

1. _____
2. _____

### LESSON 2
### ECOSYSTEMS

Definition _____
_____

Groups of Organisms in Ecosystems

1. _____
2. _____

Nonliving Parts of Ecosystems

1. _____
2. _____
3. _____
4. _____
5. _____

### LESSON 3
### HABITATS AND NICHES

Habitat _____

Niche _____

Types of Roles

1. _____
2. _____
3. _____

### LESSON 4
### TROPICAL RAIN FORESTS AND CORAL REEFS

Tropical Rain Forest _____

Description _____
_____

Homes in the Rain Forest

1. _____
2. _____

Coral Reef _____

Description _____

Homes in the Coral Reefs

1. _____

# How Parts of a System Interact

## Materials

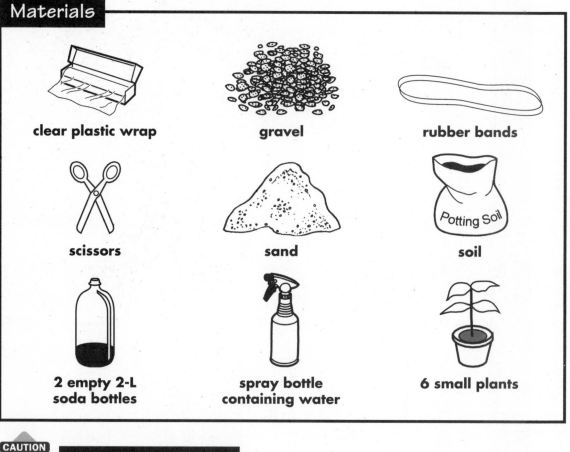

clear plastic wrap

gravel

rubber bands

scissors

sand

Potting Soil

soil

2 empty 2-L soda bottles

spray bottle containing water

6 small plants

## CAUTION  Activity Procedure

**1**  **CAUTION**  **Be careful when using scissors.** Cut the tops off the 2-L bottles.

**2**  Pour a layer of gravel in the bottom of each bottle. Cover this with a layer of sand.

**3**  Add a layer of soil to each bottle, and plant three plants in each bottle.

**4**  Spray the plants and the soil with water. Cover the tops of the bottles with plastic wrap. You may need to use the rubber bands to hold the plastic wrap in place. You have now made two examples of a system called a *terrarium* (tuh•RAIR•ee•uhm).

**5**  Put one terrarium in a sunny spot. Put the other in a dark closet or cabinet.

**6**  After three days, **observe** each terrarium and **record** what you see.

Harcourt

## Draw Conclusions

1. Which part of the system was missing from one of the terrariums?

   _____

   _____

2. What did you **observe** about the two systems? _____

   _____

   _____

   _____

3. **Scientists at Work** Scientists learn how different things interact by putting them together to form a system. What did your **model** show you about the interactions among plants, soil, air, light, and water? _____

   _____

   _____

**Investigate Further** **Hypothesize** what would happen if a terrarium had no water. Make another terrarium, but this time don't add any water. Put the terrarium in a sunny spot, and **observe** it after three days. What has happened?

   _____

   _____

   _____

Harcourt

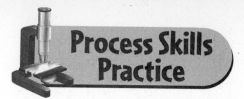

# Make a Model

In nature, systems tend to be complex. Making a model of a natural system can help you see how specific parts of that system interact.

## Think About Making a Model

Cheryl has two similar aquariums. These aquariums are the same size. Each holds four goldfish and three small aquarium plants. Cheryl decided to use one aquarium to model a sunny pond. She put it near a window that received several hours of direct sunlight daily. She put one aquarium away from windows, so it got no direct sunlight. She observed the two aquariums for a month. She recorded her observations.

| Date | Aquarium in Direct Sunlight | Aquarium Not in Direct Sunlight |
|------|------------------------------|----------------------------------|
| Nov. 5 | Fish stay in shadows of plants when sun shines directly on tank. | Fish swim throughout tank. |
| Nov. 15 | Glass is beginning to look green. Fish still avoid sun. | Aquarium glass is clear. Fish swim throughout tank. |
| Nov. 25 | Glass has green streaks, especially where sunlight strikes glass. Fish swim throughout tank. | Glass is clear. Fish swim throughout tank. |
| Dec. 5 | Glass is greener than before. Gravel and water are beginning to look green. Fish swim throughout tank. | Aquarium glass and water are clear. Fish swim throughout tank. |

1. What are the parts common to both aquarium systems? _____

   _____

   Which part was missing from one of the aquariums? _____

2. What was the main difference Cheryl observed between the two aquariums?

   _____

   _____

3. What do these models show you about the interactions among the fish, plants,

   water, gravel, and sunlight? _____

   _____

Harcourt

Name _____

Date _____

# What Are Systems?

Systems, including natural systems, have different parts that interact.

### Vocabulary

| | |
|---|---|
| **system** (B6) | **stability** (B8) |

Below is a picture of a yard system. Describe this system by filling in the chart.

| System Parts | Examples |
|---|---|
| Living parts | |
| Nonliving parts | |
| Inputs | |
| Outputs | |
| Patterns of short-term change | |
| Long-term stability | |

Harcourt

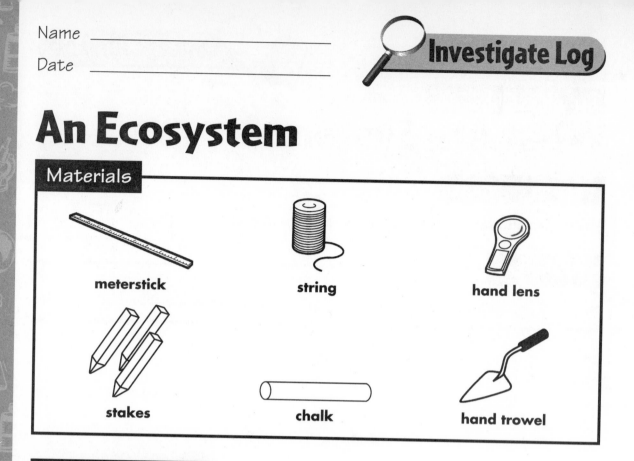
# An Ecosystem

## Materials

meterstick

string

hand lens

stakes

chalk

hand trowel

## Activity Procedure

**1** Use the meterstick to **measure** a square area that is 1 m long and 1 m wide. It can be on grass, bare dirt, or the cracked concrete of a wall or sidewalk. Mark the edges of the square with the chalk or with the stakes and string.

**2** **Observe** your study area. Look for plants and animals that live there. Use the hand lens. **Record** all the living things you see. Describe any signs that other living things have been there.

**3** *In soil or grass,* use the trowel to turn over a small area of soil. Look for insects or other living things. **Count** and **record** any living things you find. Then **classify** them. Be sure to fill in the holes you dig in your area.

**4** *In concrete or brick areas,* **observe** areas along the sides of the concrete or bricks that may contain soil and places for plants to grow. **Count** and **record** the number of each type of living thing you find. Then **classify** each.

**5** **Communicate** your results to your class. Describe your study area. Identify the living things you found.

Harcourt

Name _____

## Draw Conclusions

1. What living things did you find in your study area? _____

_____

_____

_____

Which kind of living thing was most common in your area?

_____

_____

_____

2. How was your study area different from those of other student groups?

_____

_____

_____

3. **Scientists at Work**  Scientists often **observe** an ecosystem at different times of the day and in different seasons. This is because different animals can be seen at different times. **Predict** the different animals you might see if you observed your study area at different times of the day or at different times of the year.

_____

_____

_____

_____

**Investigate Further**  Choose an area that is like the area you **observed.** Repeat the investigation. What was the same? _____

_____

What was different? _____

_____

Why were there differences? _____

_____

_____

Harcourt

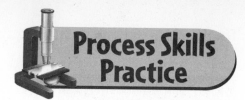

# Observe

Observing includes using all of your senses to notice things around you.

## Think About Observing

Raj knew that ecosystems like his backyard change from day to night. He wondered what this ecosystem was like at night. Raj decided to observe this ecosystem. He took a flashlight, a pencil, and a notebook and went out in his backyard after dark. He heard sounds right away. He heard the wind blowing through the leaves, a dog barking, crickets chirping, and rustling in the raspberry patch.

Raj took his flashlight and quietly walked over to investigate the raspberry patch. He turned the flashlight on. Staring back at him was a family of raccoons. He slowly backed away from the raspberry patch so the mother raccoon wouldn't be startled.

Raj slapped at the mosquitoes buzzing and trying to bite him. He looked up at the sky. The stars were shining. He heard a bird call out and saw it soaring high overhead. He thought he saw other birds flying, too, in a swooping, fluttery flight. He tried to shine his flashlight on them. But they were too dark and moved too fast for him to see well.

**1.** What were the different animals Raj observed? _____

_____

**2.** What senses did Raj rely on to make his observations? _____

_____

**3.** Which sense do you think was most important in making these observations? Explain your answer. _____

_____

_____

_____

**4.** Soon after Raj saw the bird, he had to go back inside. If he wanted to check in the morning for signs of nighttime activity, what do you think he should look

for? _____

_____

_____

Harcourt

**Use with page B11.**

Name _____

Date _____

# What Makes Up an Ecosystem?

## Lesson Concept

An ecosystem is made up of groups of living things and their environment.

## Vocabulary

**ecosystem** (B12)      **population** (B13)      **community** (B14)

**Write the letter of the best answer on the line.**

**1.** An ecosystem is made up of different species of living things _____.
   **A** called a population          **C** and the environment
   **B** called an estuary            **D** and sunlight

**2.** In an ecosystem all living things _____.
   **A** have unusual adaptations     **C** grow quickly
   **B** grow slowly                  **D** can meet their basic needs

**3.** All ecosystems contain populations of different organisms; a population is a group of _____.
   **A** the same species living in the same place at the same time
   **B** the same species living in the same place throughout the species' history
   **C** different species living in the same place at the same time

**4.** Mangrove trees are adapted to live in an ecosystem where _____.
   **A** water is scarce              **C** there is very deep water
   **B** saltiness of the water varies widely  **D** clarity of the water varies widely

**5.** Ecosystems contain communities, in which _____.
   **A** different populations compete for limited resources
   **B** different populations depend on one another for survival
   **C** organisms of a single population compete with each other for resources

**6.** The important nonliving parts of an ecosystem include air, water, soil, _____.
   **A** sunlight, and temperature     **C** heat, and carbon
   **B** salt, and sunlight            **D** shade, and bacteria

Harcourt

**Use with page B17.**

Name _____

Date _____

# The Homes and Roles of Living Things

## Materials

**index cards**

**reference books about animals**

**crayons or markers**

## Activity Procedure

**1** Each member of your group should choose five different animals.

**2** Draw a picture of each of your animals on a separate index card.

**3** Using five more cards, draw the homes of your animals or show them in their roles. Look up information about your animals in reference books if you need help.

**4** Gather all the cards. Mix up the cards, and place them face down. Take turns playing Concentration®. Turn over two cards at a time until you find a pair that shows an animal and its home or role. Explain how the two cards match. Play until all the matches have been made.

Harcourt

Name _____

## Draw Conclusions

1. What new animals did you learn about as you played the game?

_____

_____

_____

_____

2. Which was easier to identify, an animal's home or its role? Explain your answer.

_____

_____

_____

_____

3. **Scientists at Work** Scientists often make **inferences** based on things they have **observed** and their past experiences. What inferences did you make as you tried to explain how two cards matched? _____

_____

_____

_____

_____

**Investigate Further** Choose an animal card, and think of another animal that may have the same home or role. If the animals live in the same community, will they try to eat the same food or use the same places for shelter?

_____

_____

_____

Will the new animal keep the animal on the card from meeting its needs?

_____

_____

_____

Harcourt

Name _____

Date _____

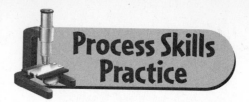

# Infer

Inferring involves explaining something based on observations you
have made and information you already know.

## Think About Inferring

Below are pictures of animals and animal homes. Match the animals to their
homes. Then answer the questions about how you came up with your matches.

**1.** platypus

**A**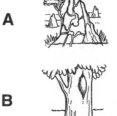

**2.** termite

**B**

**3.** bat

**C**

**1.** _____ platypus's home

How did you infer this? _____

_____

_____

_____

**2.** _____ termite's home

How did you infer this? _____

_____

_____

**3.** _____ bat's home

How did you infer this? _____

_____

_____

Harcourt

Name _____

Date _____

# What Are Habitats and Niches?

## Lesson Concept

Each living thing in an ecosystem has a habitat and a niche.

### Vocabulary

**habitat** (B20)  **niche** (B21)  **producer** (B21)

**consumer** (B21)  **decomposer** (B21)

**Read the paragraphs below about earthworms, and answer the questions that follow.**

Earthworms tunnel through the soil. They eat rotting leaves and other plant parts that fall on the ground. They also eat the remains of dead insects and other small organisms. Their waste products, called castings, add nutrients to the soil. Earthworms dig burrows for shelter and nesting. They bring leaves from the surface down into their burrows, to line their homes.

Earthworms are food for many different animals. Birds are earthworms' main above-ground predators. Some kinds of turtles, frogs, toads, and snakes also prey on earthworms. Below the ground, moles are earthworms' main predators. People catch earthworms to use as bait for fish.

1. Describe the earthworm's habitat. _____

_____

2. List three facts about the earthworm's niche. _____

_____

_____

_____

_____

3. What kind of animal is the earthworm—a producer, a consumer, or a decomposer? Explain your answer. _____

_____

Harcourt

# A Coral Reef

## Materials

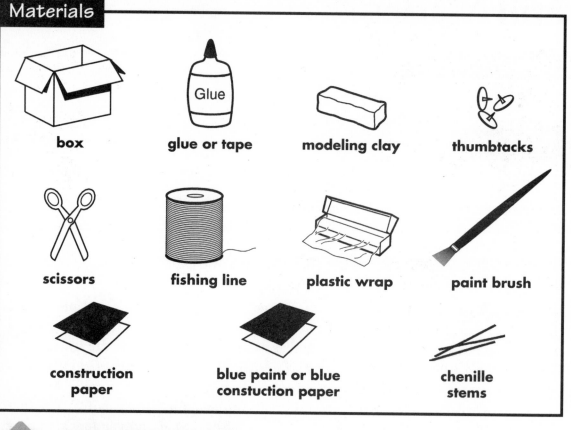

box

glue or tape

modeling clay

thumbtacks

scissors

fishing line

plastic wrap

paint brush

construction paper

blue paint or blue constuction paper

chenille stems

 **CAUTION**

## Activity Procedure

**1** Look through the lesson, and use library resources to find pictures of reef organisms and their habitats.

**2** Plan a diorama that uses the materials your teacher provides. Try to find the best material for each living and nonliving thing you will show.

**3** Follow your plan. Keep in mind colors, sizes, and the best use of space.

**4** Label the organisms in your diorama.

Harcourt

Name _____

## Draw Conclusions

1. What organisms did you include in your diorama? _____

_____

_____

_____

2. Tell three things you learned while building your diorama.

_____

_____

_____

_____

3. **Scientists at Work** When scientists build a **model** of an organism that is very small, they may make it hundreds of times bigger. If you tried to build your diorama to scale, you may have found it hard to show the very smallest organisms. How could you show large models of the tiniest organisms and still build your diorama to scale? _____

_____

_____

_____

_____

**Investigate Further** A diorama can show only part of the picture. Write a paragraph or two describing other organisms that could live near your reef scene.

_____

_____

_____

_____

_____

_____

_____

_____

_____

Harcourt

Name _____

Date _____

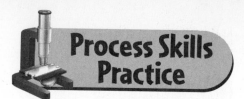

# Make a Model

Models can show relationships among different organisms in an ecosystem.

### Think About Making a Model

Keisha wanted to make a model of a nest of leaf-cutting ants. The ants eat fungi they grow in their gardens. These ants bite off small bits of leaves and take these leaf bits back to their underground nest. They chew up the leaf bits into a pulp and spread the pulp on their fungi garden. The green pulp makes the garden grow.

Keisha wanted to make her model larger than life-size so people could see details of the nest's structure and of the ants themselves. Leaf-cutting ants are usually less than 3 millimeters long. The leaf bits they cut may be up to four times that size.

**1.** If Keisha wanted to make her model in a box that measures 50 centimeters by 75 centimeters (about 20 in. × 30 in.), what do you think would be a good size to make the ants? Why would this be a good size? _____

_____

_____

**2.** How big should she make the leaf bits that the ants are carrying?

_____

_____

**3.** How could Keisha show that the nest of the leaf-cutting ants is underground?

_____

_____

**4.** If she wanted to show that the model is bigger than life-size, list two different things she could include in the diorama to give people looking at it a sense of scale. _____

_____

_____

_____

_____

Harcourt

# What Are Tropical Rain Forests and Coral Reefs?

**Lesson Concept**

Tropical rain forests and coral reefs are ecosystems that provide habitats to a large variety of plants and animals.

**Vocabulary**

| **climate** (B26) | **diversity** (B27) | **salinity** (B28) |
|---|---|---|

Fill in the chart below that compares a tropical rain forest to a coral reef.

| Characteristic of Ecosystem | Tropical Rain Forest | Coral Reef |
|---|---|---|
| Location | | |
| Temperature range | | |
| Amount of sunlight | | |
| Main type of organism | | |
| Other organisms | | |
| Habitats | | |
| Resources we get from the ecosystem | | |

**Vocabulary Review**

# Recognize Vocabulary

**Use the clues to fill in the word puzzle.**

**Across**

3. environment that meets the needs of an organism

6. over time changes cancel each other out

8. group of living things and the environment that they live in

9. organism that makes its own food

10. amount of salt in a liquid

11. all populations living in the same area

12. organism that feeds on the wastes or remains of living things

**Down**

1. role of a living thing in its habitat

2. variety of living things

4. an organism that eats other living things

5. average temperature and rainfall

6. group of parts that work together

7. group of the same species living in the same place at the same time

**Use with pages B4–B31.**

# Chapter 2 • Graphic Organizer for Chapter Concepts

## Soil—A Natural Resource

### LESSON 1
### SOIL FORMATION

**Processes That Form Soil**

1. _____

2. _____

**Three Layers of Soil**

1. _____

2. _____

3. _____

### LESSON 2
### PROPERTIES OF SOIL

**Properties of Soil**

1. _____

2. _____

3. _____

4. _____

**Types of Soil Texture**

1. _____

2. _____

3. _____

4. _____

5. _____

### LESSON 3
### CONSERVING SOIL

**Where Soils are Lost**

1. _____

2. _____

**Ways To Control Soil Loss**

1. _____

2. _____

3. _____

**Ways To Control Nutrient Loss**

1. _____

2. _____

Harcourt

# Soil Layers

## Materials

newspaper

soil sample

Potting Soil

water

hand lens

wide-mouth glass or
plastic jar with lid

## Activity Procedure

**1** Cover your work surface with newspaper.

**2** Examine the soil sample with a hand lens. Look for differences in the particles that make up soil. **Record** your **observations.**

**3** Add soil to the jar until it is about one-third full.

**4** Add water until the jar is almost full.

**5** Tightly screw the lid onto the jar. Shake the jar for at least 15 seconds to mix the soil and water well.

**6** Let the jar sit overnight.

**7** **Observe** the soil and water in the jar. Use the hand lens to observe each soil part in the jar more closely. **Record** your observations.

**My observations:** _____

_____

_____

_____

Name _____

## Draw Conclusions

1. How did mixing and shaking change the soil? _____

   _____

   _____

2. **Compare** your **observations** of the soil before shaking and after settling. In which observation could you see soil parts more easily? Explain your answer.

   _____

   _____

3. **Scientists at Work** Scientists often use instruments, or tools, to **observe** details.

   How did the hand lens help you in this investigation? _____

   _____

   _____

**Investigate Further** Soil particles can be classified by size into four groups. The groups, in order from largest to smallest, are gravel, sand, silt, and clay. Look again at the layers in the jar. Which layer contains which particle? Draw a picture of the layers, and label them.

Name _____

Date _____

# Observe

When you observe, you look for main features and details of an object or area.

## Think About Observing

**Observe the picture of soil layers, and answer the questions.**

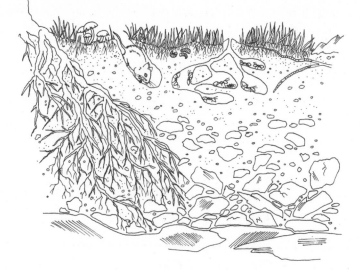

1. When you first looked at the picture of soil layers, what were three main things you noticed? _____

   _____

   _____

   _____

2. What are the nonliving things you see in the soil? What pattern do you notice in the arrangements of these things within the soil layers?

   _____

   _____

3. What are the different living things you see in the soil? What patterns do you notice in the arrangement of these organisms within the soil layers?

   _____

   _____

   _____

Harcourt

**Use with page B41.**

# How Does Soil Form?

**Lesson Concept**

Soil is important for all living things. It forms very slowly.

**Vocabulary**

| | | |
|---|---|---|
| **weathering** (B43) | **erosion** (B43) | **humus** (B44) |

Write labels for the soil diagram. In the numbered spaces below, describe the labeled layers.

_____ **1.** ⟶

_____ **2.** ⟶

_____ **3.** ⟶

**1.** _____

_____

_____

**2.** _____

_____

**3.** _____

_____

**4.** Describe ways weathering and erosion contribute to soil formation.

_____

_____

_____

_____

Harcourt

# The Ability of Soils to Hold Water

## Materials

3 clear plastic cups    wax pencil    metric ruler    2 large coffee filters

measuring cup    stir stick or spoon    water    stopwatch or watch with a second hand

2 rubber bands    $\frac{3}{4}$ cup potting soil    $\frac{1}{4}$ cup sand

## Activity Procedure

1 Use the chart on the next page.

2 On each cup, mark lines 1 cm, 2 cm, 3 cm, and 4 cm from the bottom. Label one cup *Potting Soil*, label another cup *Sandy Soil*, and label the last cup *Water*.

3 Put a coffee filter over the top of the potting-soil cup. With your fingertips, push it about halfway into the cup. Fold the filter edge over the rim of the cup. Use a rubber band to hold the filter on the cup.

4 Repeat Step 3 for the sandy-soil cup.

5 Pour $\frac{1}{2}$ cup of potting soil into the coffee filter of the potting-soil cup.

6 Pour the sand into the remaining potting soil. Stir it well to make sandy soil. Pour $\frac{1}{2}$ cup of sandy soil into the coffee filter of the sandy-soil cup.

7 **Predict** whether sandy soil or potting soil will drain water faster. **Record** your prediction.

Harcourt

**Investigate Log**

**8** Fill the water cup up to the 4-cm mark.
Pour the water into the potting-soil cup. As you start to pour, have a partner start the stopwatch. **Record** the time when water begins dripping through the filter. Also record the time when the water stops dripping. Then record the amount of water in the bottom of the cup.

**9** Repeat Step 8 for the sandy soil.

| Soil Types and Water Drainage | | |
|---|---|---|
| | **Potting Soil** | **Sandy Soil** |
| Time of first drop | | |
| Time of last drop | | |
| Amount of water drained | | |

## Draw Conclusions

**1.** Which soil type held water longer? _____

Was your prediction correct? _____

**2.** Which soil type do you **infer** would be better for planting a cactus?

_____

Why? _____

_____

**3. Scientists at Work** When scientists **control variables**, they can find out the effect of one change. List the variables in this experiment.

_____

_____

Which variable was changed? _____

Which variables stayed the same? _____

_____

**Investigate Further** Repeat this activity for several soil types. You can use soils you can buy, soil from your yard, or your own soil mixes. How did the different types hold water? _____

_____

Harcourt

Name _____

Date _____

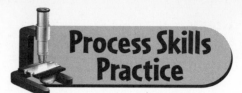

# Identify and Control Variables

Variables are factors that affect how an experiment works. Controlling variables is important for running an experiment.

## Think About Identifying and Controlling Variables

Felipé works at a greenhouse. His boss wants him to grow ficus trees. But he doesn't know which type of soil ficus trees grow best in. So Felipé decides to conduct an experiment to see how different soils affect the growth of ficus trees.

**1.** What variable should he change when he does this experiment?

_____

**2.** What variables should not be changed? List as many as you can think of.

_____

_____

_____

_____

**3.** Why is it important that Felipé keep the variables listed in Question 2 the same for all of the plants? _____

_____

_____

**4.** Felipé's results show that the trees grow better in potting soil than in sandy soil or in clay soil. Do you think his results would have been the same if he used pots that drained different amounts of water? Describe an experiment he could do to find out. Identify the variables he should control and the variable he should change. _____

_____

_____

Harcourt

# What Are Some Properties of Soil?

## Lesson Concept

Soil properties make some soil types better than others for growing plants.

## Vocabulary

**fertile** (B50)

**Fill in the diagram to list the important properties of soil, and explain why each is important to plants.**

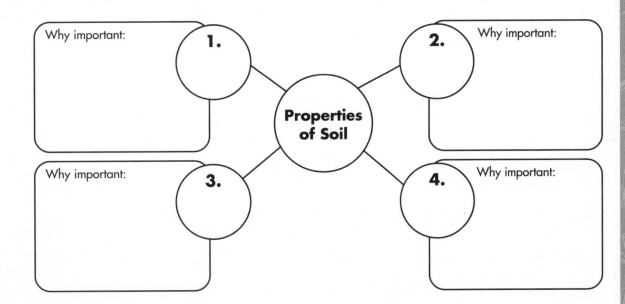

**5.** What can people do to improve soil lacking nutrients? Give examples.

_____

_____

_____

_____

# Soil Erosion

## Materials

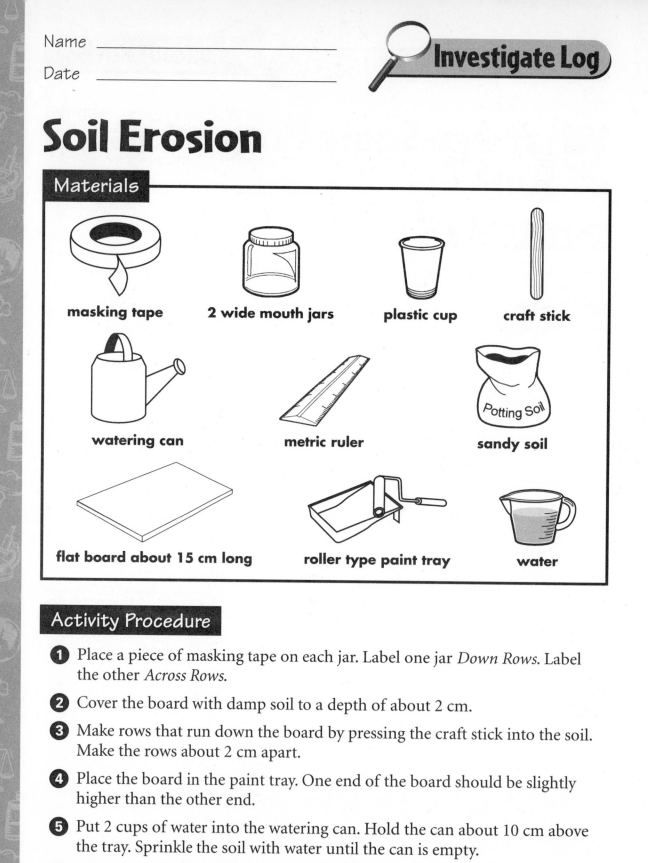

masking tape

2 wide mouth jars

plastic cup

craft stick

watering can

metric ruler

sandy soil

flat board about 15 cm long

roller type paint tray

water

## Activity Procedure

1. Place a piece of masking tape on each jar. Label one jar *Down Rows*. Label the other *Across Rows*.

2. Cover the board with damp soil to a depth of about 2 cm.

3. Make rows that run down the board by pressing the craft stick into the soil. Make the rows about 2 cm apart.

4. Place the board in the paint tray. One end of the board should be slightly higher than the other end.

5. Put 2 cups of water into the watering can. Hold the can about 10 cm above the tray. Sprinkle the soil with water until the can is empty.

6. Carefully remove the board and set it aside. Pour the runoff from the paint tray into the *Down Rows* jar.

Harcourt

**7** Smooth out the soil on the board.
Add soil to make the depth about 2 cm. Make fresh rows in the soil, only this time make rows that run across the board.

**8** Repeat Steps 4–6, but pour the runoff water into the *Across Rows* jar.

**9** Allow the soil in both jars to settle for 30 minutes.

## Draw Conclusions

1. **Observe** the material in each jar. Which jar has more runoff?

_____

_____

Which jar has more soil? _____

_____

2. Which model showed the better way to keep soil from eroding?

_____

3. **Scientists at Work** Scientists **compare** results of tests to find the best answer.

What did you compare in this activity? _____

_____

**Investigate Further** See how covering soil affects the amount of runoff and soil erosion. Repeat the experiment, but this time cover the soil with shredded newspaper. Use different jars to collect runoff. Which material had the least runoff? Use your data to **draw a conclusion** about how soil cover affects the

amount of runoff and soil erosion. _____

_____

_____

_____

_____

Harcourt

Process Skills
Practice

# Compare

Comparing involves noting things that are alike and different. You compare
when you identify similarities and differences among results of an experiment.

## Think About Comparing

Tiffany wanted to see how covering soil affects a sample exposed to high winds.
She made a model of two flat fields by filling two cake pans with soil. In one of the
pans, she planted grass seed; the other pan held only the soil. After the grass was
about 1 in. tall, Tiffany began her experiment.
She pushed one end of a table against a wall
and taped a big sheet of paper labeled *Bare Soil*
to the table and to the wall. Then she took a
powerful fan and directed it to blow right
across the surface of the soil. She let the fan
blow for one minute. Then she carefully
untaped the paper from the wall and the table,
folding it so that the loose soil stayed in the fold
of the paper. She taped up another sheet of
paper labeled *Grass-covered Soil* and repeated
her procedure exactly as she had done for the
pan with bare soil. She weighed and recorded
the amounts of soil caught by each sheet of paper. Then she compared the weights.

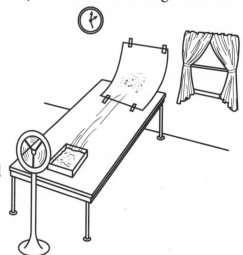

1. What was Tiffany comparing in this experiment? _____

   _____

   _____

2. After Tiffany completed her experiment, she observed that much more soil had
   collected on the paper labeled *Bare Soil* than had collected on the paper labeled
   *Grass-Covered Soil*. What conclusion could she draw by comparing these

   results? _____

3. Tiffany also noticed that the bare soil was dryer than the soil that was planted
   with grass. How might she use this comparison to improve her experiment?

   _____

   _____

Harcourt

Name _____

Date _____

Concept Review

# What Are Some Ways to Conserve Soil?

## Lesson Concept

Soil loss causes problems. There are many ways people can prevent soil loss.

## Vocabulary

**soil conservation** (B56)    **contour plowing** (B56)    **strip cropping** (B56)
**terracing** (B56)

**Answer the questions about soil conservation below.**

**1.** What are two negative things that happen when soil washes into a river?

_____

_____

**2.** Describe one positive thing that can happen when soil washes into a river.

_____

_____

**Describe three ways farmers conserve soil.**

**3.** _____

_____

**4.** _____

_____

**5.** _____

_____

**6.** What is one way farmers can prevent the loss of many nutrients from the

soil? _____

_____

_____

Harcourt

# Recognize Vocabulary

**Each definition is incorrect. Write the correct definition on the line below the term.**

1. **contour plowing**: using a shovel to landscape a flower garden

   _____

2. **erosion**: the process by which wind pushes water up a hill

   _____

3. **fertile**: how far a rock can be thrown

   _____

4. **humus**: vegetable used in sandwiches

   _____

5. **soil conservation**: a place where soil is allowed to roam free in its natural

   habitat _____

6. **strip cropping**: pulling up all the crops in a field to harvest them

   _____

7. **terracing**: using a flat rock to make the bottom of terra-cotta pots

   _____

8. **weathering**: rock is exposed to different weather conditions

   _____

Harcourt

# Chapter 3 • Graphic Organizer for Chapter Concepts

## Protecting Ecosystems

### LESSON 1
### ECOSYSTEM CHANGES

**Slow Changes**

1. _____

2. _____

3. _____

**Rapid Changes**

1. _____

2. _____

3. _____

### LESSON 2
### HUMAN INTERACTIONS WITH ECOSYSTEMS

**Damage Humans Cause**

1. _____

2. _____

**Things That Help Repair Ecosystems**

1. _____

2. _____

3. _____

### LESSON 3
### CONSERVING ECOSYSTEMS

**Conserving Resources**

1. _____

2. _____

3. _____

**Preserving Resources**

1. _____

2. _____

3. _____

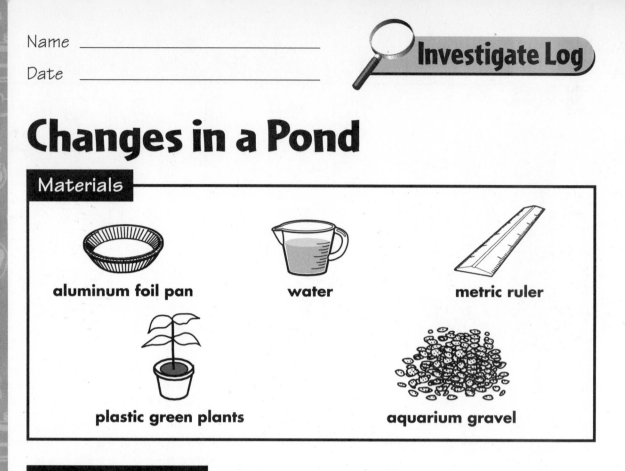
# Changes in a Pond

## Materials

aluminum foil pan

water

metric ruler

plastic green plants

aquarium gravel

## Activity Procedure

**1** Use the chart below. **Make a model** of a pond that has formed in a low spot on exposed rock. Fill the pan half-full of water.

| Investigation Step | Measurement of Water's Surface | Observations |
|---|---|---|
| Step 2 | | |
| Step 4 | | |
| Step 5 | | |

Harcourt

**Investigate Log**

**2** **Measure** and **record** the distance across the water's surface. Try to "plant" a few plants near the sides of your pond. Record your **observations**.

**3** **Predict** what will happen to the pond if you add gravel and then plants.

**My predictions:** _____

**4** Slowly add gravel to your model pond. The gravel stands for soil that has washed into the pond during 200 years. In a real pond more soil builds up around the edges than in the middle. Put more gravel around the edges of the pond than in the middle. **Measure** and **record** the distance across the water's surface. Again "plant" several plants near the sides of the pond. Record your **observations**.

**5** Add more gravel and plants until you can no longer see the water's surface. This represents several hundred years of adding soil. **Record** your **observations** of what was once a pond.

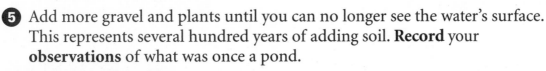

## Draw Conclusions

1. Describe how your pond changed over time. _____
   _____
   _____
   _____

2. As a pond changes, how might the living things in it change? Explain your answer. _____
   _____
   _____
   _____

3. **Scientists at Work** When you **observed** your pond model, you **collected data.** What does your data tell you about how a natural pond changes over time?
   _____
   _____
   _____

**Investigate Further** Ponds go through *stages*, or steps, as they get older. Draw a picture showing four stages of a pond. Label the stages *new pond, old pond, marsh,* and *meadow*.

Harcourt

Name _____

Date _____

# Collect Data

When you collect data, you make observations and measurements and record them in an organized way.

## Think About Collecting Data

Ian lives in an area where there are many farms, meadows, and forests. He has noticed that every year certain changes occur in the countryside around him. These changes mark the seasons. Ian wants to keep track of when these seasonal changes happen in different years.

1. Ian is trying to set up an observation journal. In this journal he wants to record the dates that specific changes occur for at least the next two years. Ian also wants to record specific observations he makes on specific dates. Which of the following kinds of record books do you think would work best for Ian? Explain your answer.

_____

_____

_____

_____

2. During the spring Ian noticed wildflowers in the woods for a few weeks. He decided to keep track of the number of different kinds of wildflowers he saw in the woods during the spring months. Describe a way he might collect this data. Tell how he could compare this data for two different years.

_____

_____

_____

_____

Harcourt

**Concept Review**

# What Kinds of Changes Occur in Ecosystems?

## Lesson Concept

Ecosystems change due to natural and human-made causes.

## Vocabulary

**succession** (B70)

1. What are big changes that occur over time in ecosystems called? What can cause these big changes? _____

    _____

2. Name three types of rapid changes that occur naturally in ecosystems.

    _____

    _____

    _____

3. Describe one type of rapid change that people cause in ecosystems.

    _____

    _____

4. List ways that people protect themselves during rapid changes in ecosystems.

    _____

    _____

    _____

    _____

Harcourt

# Cleaning Up Pond Pollution

## Materials

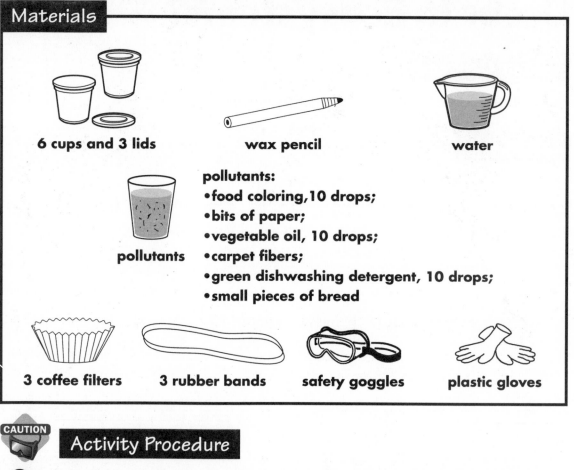

6 cups and 3 lids     wax pencil     water

pollutants

pollutants:
- food coloring, 10 drops;
- bits of paper;
- vegetable oil, 10 drops;
- carpet fibers;
- green dishwashing detergent, 10 drops;
- small pieces of bread

3 coffee filters     3 rubber bands     safety goggles     plastic gloves

## CAUTION Activity Procedure

1. Label one cup *Pollutant 1*, a second cup *Pollutant 2*, and a third *Pollutant 3*.

2. Label one of the other three cups *Filtered pollutant 1*, the second *Filtered pollutant 2*, and the third *Filtered pollutant 3*. You should now have three pairs of cups.

3. Fill each of the three pollutant cups half-full of water. **CAUTION Put on the safety goggles and plastic gloves.** Put two different pollutants in each cup. Put the lids on tightly, and shake each cup well.

4. **Observe** one of the cups that contain polluted water. **Record** what you see.

   **My observations:** _____

   _____

Harcourt

**5** Push a clean coffee filter halfway into the *Filtered pollutant 1* cup. Put a rubber band around the top of the cup to hold the filter in place. Pour about half of the *Pollutant 1* water into the filter.

**6** When the water has drained, **compare** the filtered water with the polluted water. **Record** your observations.

My observations: _____

_____

**7** Repeat Steps 4–6 for the other two cups of polluted water.

My observations: _____

_____

## Draw Conclusions

**1.** How were the mixtures you filtered alike? _____

_____

**2.** Which pollutants were filtered out? _____

_____

**3. Scientists at Work** Scientists **compare** samples to find the smallest differences. How did the polluted water containing oil look compared to the filtered water?

_____

_____

How did the filtered detergent mixture compare to the mixture before it was

filtered? _____

_____

**Investigate Further** Sand is sometimes used as a filter to clean water for drinking. Fill a cup with water. Add a spoonful of flour or baby powder. Stir well. Plug the end of a funnel with one or two cotton balls. Fill the funnel half-full of clean sand. Put the funnel into a jar. Pour the mixture of water and powder into the funnel.

**Observe** the filtered water. How well did the sand work? _____

_____

_____

How do you know? _____

Harcourt

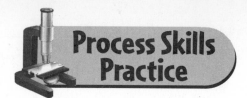

# Compare

Comparing involves noting differences between two situations or two objects.

## Think About Comparing

Compare the pictures of the backyard drawn ten years apart. Circle the things in the second picture of the backyard that are different from the first picture.

**May, 1990**

**May, 2000**

Pick three of the changes in this backyard. Tell how each change may help living things that live in or near the backyard.

**Change 1:** _____

How it helps living things: _____

_____

**Change 2:** _____

How it helps living things: _____

_____

_____

**Change 3:** _____

How it helps living things: _____

_____

Harcourt

# How Do People Change Ecosystems?

## Lesson Concept

People can cause both harmful and beneficial changes to ecosystems.

## Vocabulary

reclamation (B80)

Fill in the chart to describe how people affect ecosystems and how they can repair or help ecosystems.

| What People Do | Effects on Ecosystem | Ways to Help Ecosystem |
|---|---|---|
| Spray chemicals on farmland. | 1. | 2. |
| Build dams on rivers. | 3. | 4. |
| Collect coral from reefs. | 5. | 6. |
| Cut down all trees in rain forest. | 7. | 8. |

**Answer the question below.**

**9.** What reclamation is done today to repair damage caused by strip mining?

_____

_____

_____

_____

Harcourt

# Using Our National Parks

## Materials

**7 index cards**

**yarn**

**tape recorder or video camera (optional)**

## Activity Procedure

**1** Work with six other students. Each member of your group should role-play one of the following people:

Ten-year-old park visitor     Scientist who studies park plants

Adult park visitor     Local member of Congress

Park ranger     Reporter

Souvenir-shop owner

**2** Use the index cards and yarn to make a name tag for each group member. Use the names on the list in Step 1.

**3** Below are some questions about protecting national parks. Think about how the person you are role-playing views each question. Discuss the questions with your group. Work to agree on ways to help national parks.

• Should we limit the number of people who can visit a park at any one time?

• Should we make people park their cars outside the parks and have them use buses or trains instead?

• Should we reduce the number of restaurants, snack bars, shops, and gas stations in the parks?

• Should we limit activities that harm living things in the parks, such as hiking off marked trails?

• Should we spend more money to study how to preserve national parks?

• Should we provide money to educate people about the value of national parks and about ways to keep parks healthy?

**4** Use a tape recorder or a video camera to record the discussion. Review the tape to make detailed notes.

Name _____

## Investigate Log

### Draw Conclusions

1. Based on your discussion, **record** one or more ways to protect our national parks. Everyone in the group should agree to each way. Give reasons to support each idea. _____

   _____

   _____

   _____

2. To make your final decision, did anyone have to give up something that he or she wanted? If so, what? _____

   _____

3. **Scientists at Work** Scientists **communicate** with one another to find out new ideas. Were you respectful of one another's ideas and opinions? Did too many people try to talk at once? How could your group communicate better?

   _____

   _____

   _____

**Investigate Further** Make a list of the solutions your group agreed to. Find out if any of the national parks have made or plan to make these changes.

_____

_____

_____

_____

_____

_____

_____

_____

Harcourt

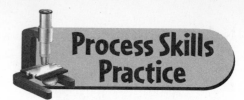

# Communicate

Communicating involves both giving and receiving information.

## Think About Communicating

A mining company discovered a deposit of coal beneath productive farmland. The town near this farmland is growing fast and many people are moving there. The landowner, a representative of the mining company, and two town residents are discussing what they think should be done with the land.

> I'm the landowner. This is excellent farmland that produces a lot of food from this area.
> —Landowner

> I'm from the mining company, and I want to buy this land. The grain on this land is only worth $500 per acre, but the coal is worth $200,000 per acre. We would mine this land and put a park in its place.
> —Mining Company Representative

> I'm a local resident. I think it's a bad idea. The amount of good farmland is decreasing in this country. This land could never be farmed again, and we will miss it in the future if Earth's population doesn't stop growing.
> —Local Resident

> I'm another local resident. I think the landowner would be a fool not to take your offer. This town is growing, and the people moving in need jobs. And we could really use another park.
> —Local Resident #2

**1.** An argument is a statement someone makes to convince others to choose an option. Which of these four people is not making an argument? Explain.

_____

_____

**2.** What might be wrong with the argument from the local resident who is in favor of selling the land? _____

_____

_____

**3.** Do you think the landowner should sell the land? Why or why not?

_____

_____

Harcourt

**Concept Review**

# What Is Conservation?

## Lesson Concept

We need to conserve our resources to protect ecosystems and meet our needs in the future.

## Vocabulary

**conservation** (B86)                    **preservation** (B88)

**Write the letter of the best answer on the lines.**

1. What do ecosystems provide for us? _____
   **A** wood for furniture and paper      **C** water for drinking and bathing
   **B** land for homes and growing food   **D** all of them

2. The careful management and wise use of natural resources is called _____.
   **A** reclamation    **B** conservation    **C** preservation    **D** communication

3. Three ways of reducing trash are to recycle materials, _____.
   **A** pick up litter off the street, and reuse things
   **B** buy products that have less packaging, and pick up litter off the street
   **C** reuse things, and buy products that have less packaging

4. What does recycling involve? _____
   **A** lining trash cans with old shopping bags
   **B** processing unused materials
   **C** processing used materials

5. When people protect an ecosystem from change by putting limits on its use, the ecosystem is being _____.
   **A** conserved    **B** preserved    **C** replenished    **D** eroded

6. One thing people CANNOT do when they set aside an area as a national park is to _____.
   **A** stop people from changing other ecosystems
   **B** limit where people go and how people use the park
   **C** help protect unusual landscapes

Harcourt

# Recognize Vocabulary

**Write the definition of each of the vocabulary terms, and give three examples of each.**

**1. conservation**

Definition: _____

Examples: _____

_____

**2. preservation**

Definition: _____

Examples: _____

_____

**3. reclamation**

Definition: _____

Examples: _____

_____

_____

**4. succession**

Definition: _____

Examples: _____

_____

Harcourt

## Chapter 1 • Graphic Organizer for Chapter Concepts

### Earthquakes and Volcanoes

**LESSON 1**
**EARTH'S LAYERS**

Three Layers

1. _____

2. _____

3. _____

Layers that Form Plates
that Move

1. _____

2. _____

**LESSON 2**
**EARTHQUAKES**

Definition _____

Cause _____

Where Movement Occurs

_____

Point on Surface Directly Above
where Movement Occurs

_____

How measured

_____

**LESSON 3**
**VOLCANOES**

Definition _____

_____

Parts of a Volcano

1. _____

2. _____

3. _____

Types of Volcanoes

1. _____

2. _____

3. _____

How Volcanoes Change the Land

1. _____

2. _____

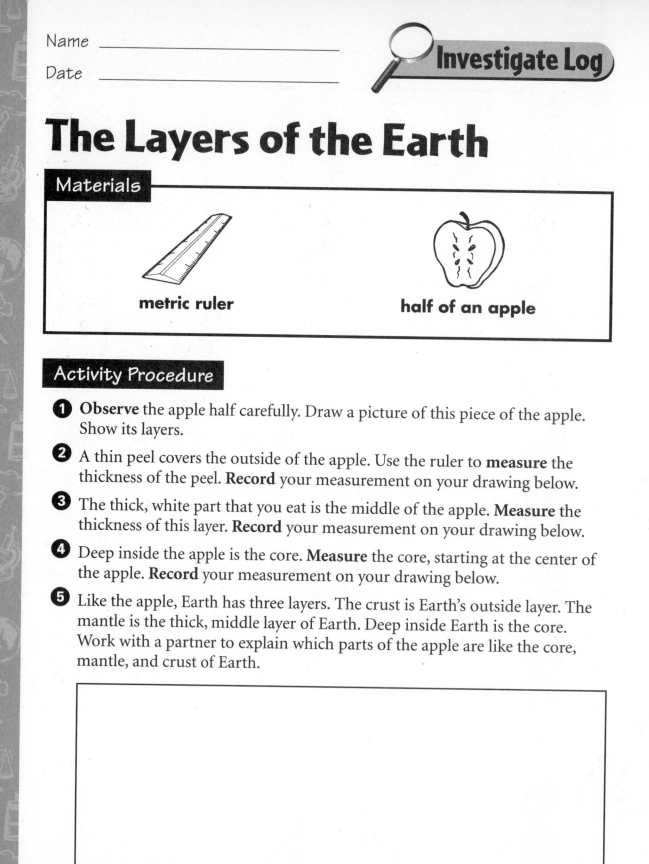
# The Layers of the Earth

## Materials

metric ruler

half of an apple

## Activity Procedure

1 **Observe** the apple half carefully. Draw a picture of this piece of the apple. Show its layers.

2 A thin peel covers the outside of the apple. Use the ruler to **measure** the thickness of the peel. **Record** your measurement on your drawing below.

3 The thick, white part that you eat is the middle of the apple. **Measure** the thickness of this layer. **Record** your measurement on your drawing below.

4 Deep inside the apple is the core. **Measure** the core, starting at the center of the apple. **Record** your measurement on your drawing below.

5 Like the apple, Earth has three layers. The crust is Earth's outside layer. The mantle is the thick, middle layer of Earth. Deep inside Earth is the core. Work with a partner to explain which parts of the apple are like the core, mantle, and crust of Earth.

Harcourt

Name _____

## Draw Conclusions

1. **Use numbers** to **compare** the layers of the apple. Which layer is the thinnest?

   _____

2. Which of Earth's layers is most like the apple peel? Explain your answer.

   _____

3. **Scientists at Work** Scientists use many kinds of tools to **measure** objects and their characteristics. How did using a ruler help you describe the apple's layers?

   _____

   _____

**Investigate Further** Use a small gum ball, modeling clay, and colored plastic wrap to make a cut-away model of Earth's layers. Which material will you use to stand

for the core? _____

Which material should you use to stand for the crust? _____

_____

For the mantle? _____

Harcourt

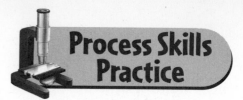

# Measure

When you use a ruler to find the height of something, you are measuring. Measuring allows you to use numbers to compare different objects in a precise manner.

## Think About Measuring

Clark's teacher asks him to compare the heights of four mountains and the depths of two valleys. He is given a picture of several mountains and valleys side by side. He is told that 1 millimeter represents 2000 meters of height on Earth's surface. The landforms in the picture are drawn to scale. Clark uses a metric ruler to measure the height and depth of each landform and fills in the table with his measurements.

**Fill in the rest of the table with the approximate heights and depths in meters.**

| Landform | Measurement on Drawing in Millimeters | Approximate Distance in Meters |
|---|---|---|
| Mount Everest | 45 high | |
| Anna Purna | 40 high | |
| Aconcagua | 35 high | |
| Mount McKinley | 30 high | |
| Puerto Rico Trough | 45 deep | |
| Marianas Trench | 55 deep | |

1. To find how much Earth's surface can vary in height and depth, Clark added the height of the tallest mountain to the depth of the deepest valley.

   What did Clark find out? _____

2. If Clark didn't use numbers, what trouble would he have when describing the

   differences between the heights of these mountains? _____

   _____

   _____

Harcourt

Name _____

Date _____

# What Are the Layers of the Earth?

## Lesson Concept

Earth is made up of three layers: the crust, the mantle, and the core.

## Vocabulary

| | | | |
|---|---|---|---|
| **crust** (C6) | **mantle** (C6) | **core** (C6) | **plate** (C8) |

Label the diagram of Earth's layers, and give a brief description of each layer.

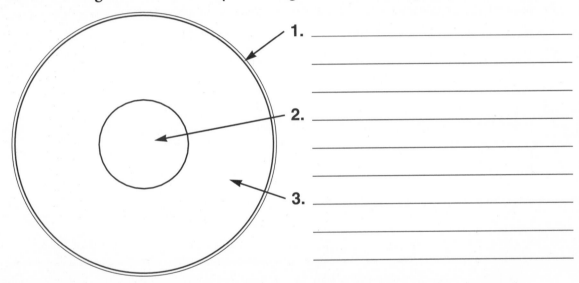

1. _____
   _____
   _____

2. _____
   _____

3. _____
   _____
   _____

Describe how the plates are moving in each diagram. Then tell where this kind of movement usually occurs and what the results are.

4. _____ 5. _____ 6. _____
   _____    _____    _____
   _____    _____    _____
   _____    _____    _____

Harcourt

# Earthquakes

## Materials

| | | |
|---|---|---|
| 3-in. × 5-in. self-stick note | small plastic cup | water |

## Activity Procedure

**1** Stick the self-stick note to a table. Be sure that about 1 in. of the short side of the self-stick note is hanging over the edge of the table. Also make sure the self-stick note is firmly stuck in place.

**2** Fill the cup $\frac{1}{4}$ full with water. Place the cup on the center part of the self-stick note that is on the table.

**3** Carefully and firmly try to pull the self-stick note straight out from under the cup. The sticky part of the note will stop you from easily pulling it all the way out. **Observe** what happens to the water.

**My observations:** _____

_____

_____

_____

_____

Harcourt

Name _____

Investigate Log

## Draw Conclusions

1.  How is snapping your fingers like the movement of the self-stick note?

    _____

    _____

    _____

    _____

    _____

2.  What did you **observe** about the water in the cup when you pulled on the

    self-stick note? _____

    _____

3.  **Scientists at Work**  Scientists often **infer** things based on their observations.
    What can you infer might happen when plates are moving past one another if

    the pressure between the plates is suddenly changed? _____

    _____

**Investigate Further**  Use two 3-in. × 5-in. self-stick notes to model two plates
sticking. Bend the notes so that the sticky parts face each other. Touch the sticky
parts together and slide one note past the other. How does the shape of the note

papers change? How do they move? _____

    _____

    _____

Harcourt

Name _____

Date _____

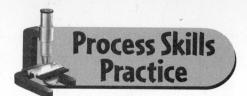

# Observe and Infer

Observing involves using your senses to notice things around you. Inferring involves using what you observe to form an opinion. For example, you can observe a glass falling and infer that it will break when it hits the ground.

## Think About Observing and Inferring

Rita learns that ocean waves caused by underwater earthquakes are called tsunamis (tsoo•NAH•meez). Tsunamis may pass through deep water unnoticed. But when tsunamis reach shallow waters near a coast, waves crest as powerful walls of water that can cause great destruction and kill people.

Rita made a table to see if earthquake strength is related to tsunami formation. She listed several famous earthquakes that occurred near large bodies of water. She recorded their strengths based on the Richter scale. On the Richter scale, higher measurements mean stronger earthquakes. Then she recorded whether or not a tsunami formed.

| Location and Year of Earthquake | Measurement on the Richter Scale | Tsunami Generated |
|---|---|---|
| New Madrid, Missouri, 1811 | approximately 7.5 | yes, on the Mississippi River |
| Owens Valley, California, 1872 | approximately 8.3 | yes, in Pacific Ocean |
| Tokyo, Japan, 1923 | approximately 8.3 | yes, in Pacific Ocean |
| Prince William Sound, Alaska, 1964 | 8.6 | yes, in Pacific Ocean |
| Southern California, 1981 | 4.8 | no |
| Long Island, New York, 1981 | 3.7 | no |

1. List two observations Rita could make about tsunamis. _____

_____

_____

2. What inference could Rita make based on the data from the table?

_____

_____

Harcourt

Name _____

Date _____

**Concept Review**

# What Causes Earthquakes?

## Lesson Concept

An earthquake is vibrations produced when energy builds up and is quickly released along a fault.

## Vocabulary

| | | |
|---|---|---|
| **earthquake** (C12) | **fault** (C12) | **focus** (C13) |
| **epicenter** (C13) | **seismograph** (C14) | |

Use the correct word from the list below to fill in the blanks.

| | | | | |
|---|---|---|---|---|
| **brick** | **faults** | **Mercalli** | **plates** | **earthquake** |
| **epicenter** | **focus** | **Richter** | **seismograph** | |

Earth's crust is broken into _____ that move relative to one

another. Breaks between plates are known as _____. Plates slide past
each other along these breaks. However, sometimes rocks from two different plates
stick together along a fault. Great pressure can build up in these rocks, and
become so great that the rocks suddenly break apart. This releases waves of energy
and causes the plates to move with a sudden jolt. We call this shaking in Earth's

crust a(n) _____.

Earthquakes usually center around a single point under Earth's surface, called

the _____. The point on Earth's surface right above this spot is the

_____.

Earthquakes are measured with an instrument called a _____.
Scientists use information from this instrument to measure the energy an
earthquake releases. They use this information to rate the earthquake on a scale,

called the _____ scale. This scale generally uses the numbers from 1 to 9,
with a thirtyfold increase in energy from one number to the next. Major earthquakes
register at 6 or higher.

Another way to measure earthquakes is by looking at the damage they cause,

using the _____ scale. This scale uses Roman numerals from I to XII. An
earthquake that measures III on this scale causes a hanging lamp to swing.

An earthquake that measures X causes _____ buildings to crumble.

Harcourt

**Use with page C15.**

**Workbook** WB111

# Volcanic Eruptions

## Materials

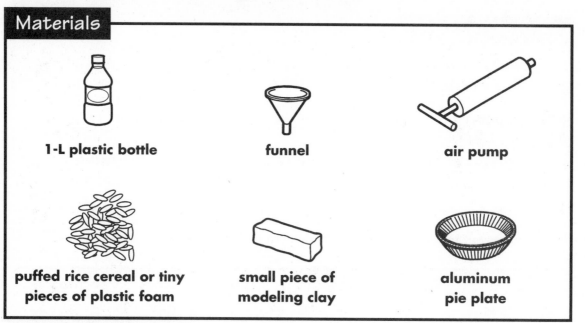

1-L plastic bottle      funnel      air pump

puffed rice cereal or tiny pieces of plastic foam      small piece of modeling clay      aluminum pie plate

## Activity Procedure

**1** Ask your teacher to make a hole near the bottom of the bottle. Use the clay to stick the bottom of the bottle to the pie plate.

**2** Use the funnel to fill the bottle $\frac{1}{4}$ full with the rice cereal or foam.

**3** Attach the air pump to the hole in the bottle. Put a piece of clay around the hole to seal it.

**4** Pump air into the bottle. **Observe** what happens.

**My observations:** _____

_____

_____

_____

_____

## Draw Conclusions

**1.** What happened to the cereal when you pumped air into the bottle?

_____

**2.** How could you make more cereal shoot out of the bottle?

_____

**3.** **Scientists at Work** Scientists often **make a model** to help them understand things that happen in nature. How is the bottle used to model an erupting

volcano? _____

_____

_____

**Investigate Further** Some volcanoes have steep sides. Others have gently sloping sides. Use some fine sand and some gravel to **make a model** of each of these two kinds of volcanoes. Make a pile of sand. Do the same with the gravel. Which model has steeper sides? How are the sand and gravel piles like volcanoes? How

are they unlike volcanoes? _____

_____

_____

_____

_____

_____

Harcourt

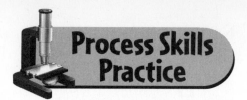

# Make a Model

Making a model can help you visualize and understand something you might have a hard time observing.

## Think About Making a Model

Thomas wanted to understand what happens when two plates move away from each other at the bottom of the Atlantic Ocean. He decided to make a model using two sponges and three different colors of modeling clay. The sponges represented the two plates. The modeling clay represented molten rock (lava) coming up through a fault and forming new crust. The pictures show how Thomas's model worked. Each of the different colors of clay represents molten rock of different ages.

**Stage 1**

**Stage 2**

**Stage 3**

**1.** Thomas made a color key like the one at the right to show the ages of the molten rock in his model. Show how you think Thomas filled in his key. (If crayons or markers are not available, write the name of the color near the box.) Color or label the layers in the model to match the key.

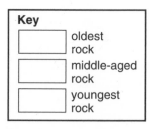

Key

☐ oldest rock

☐ middle-aged rock

☐ youngest rock

**2.** Thomas later read that scientists have mapped the ocean floor in areas where two plates are pulling apart. They have found that on both sides of the fault, the oldest rocks are farthest from the fault and the youngest rocks are closest to the fault. The rocks also form a striped pattern in terms of their magnetic properties. Based on this information, do you think Thomas's model is an

accurate one? Why or why not? _____

_____

_____

_____

Harcourt

Use with page C17.

Name _____

Date _____

# How Do Volcanoes Form?

## Lesson Concept

A volcano is a crack in Earth's crust through which lava flows out onto Earth's surface.

## Vocabulary

| | | |
|---|---|---|
| **volcano** (C18) | **magma** (C18) | **lava** (C18) |
| **vent** (C18) | **magma chamber** (C19) | **crater** (C20) |

**Answer the questions below about volcanoes.**

**1.** Describe three ways volcanoes form. _____

_____

_____

_____

_____

_____

**2.** Name three different kinds of volcanic mountains, and describe how each

forms. _____

_____

_____

_____

_____

_____

**3.** List three ways that volcanoes can be harmful. Tell how volcanic eruptions can

also be helpful. _____

_____

_____

_____

# Recognize Vocabulary

Write the letter of the best answer on the lines.

| focus | lava | fault | vent |
| plate | crust | magma | crater |
| mantle | epicenter | core | |

1. Earth's outermost layer is the _____.
   **A** core      **B** crust      **C** mantle      **D** plate

2. The middle of Earth's three layers is the _____.
   **A** core      **B** crust      **C** mantle      **D** plate

3. The innermost layer of Earth is the _____.
   **A** core      **B** crust      **C** mantle      **D** plate

4. A volcano can fall in on itself, creating a large basin called _____.
   **A** a crater      **B** an epicenter      **C** a fault      **D** a plate

5. A break in Earth's crust along which rocks move is called _____.
   **A** an earthquake   **B** an epicenter   **C** a fault   **D** a volcano

6. The point underground where earthquake's movement first takes place is called the _____.
   **A** crater      **B** epicenter      **C** fault      **D** focus

7. The point on Earth's surface right above the spot where the first movement of an earthquake occurs is called the earthquake's _____.
   **A** crater      **B** epicenter      **C** fault      **D** focus

8. Melted rock that reaches Earth's surface is called _____.
   **A** crust      **B** iron      **C** lava      **D** magma

9. Melted rock inside Earth is called _____.
   **A** crust      **B** iron      **C** lava      **D** magma

10. A _____ is the tube in a volcano that carries hot melted rock to the surface.
   **A** crater      **B** fault      **C** magma chamber   **D** vent

Harcourt

Name _____ Date _____

# Chapter 2 • Graphic Organizer for Chapter Concepts

## Rocks and Minerals

### LESSON 1
### MINERALS

How They Form

1. _____
2. _____
3. _____

Mineral Properties

1. _____
2. _____
3. _____

How They Are Used

1. _____
2. _____
3. _____
4. _____
5. _____

### LESSON 2
### ROCKS

Three Types

1. Name _____
   Form _____
   Three examples _____
2. Name _____
   Form _____
   Three examples _____
3. Name _____
   Form _____
   Three examples _____

### LESSON 3
### THE ROCK CYCLE

Definition _____
_____
_____

Processes Involved

1. _____
2. _____
3. _____
4. _____
5. _____
6. _____
7. _____

Name _____

Date _____

# Mineral Properties

## Materials

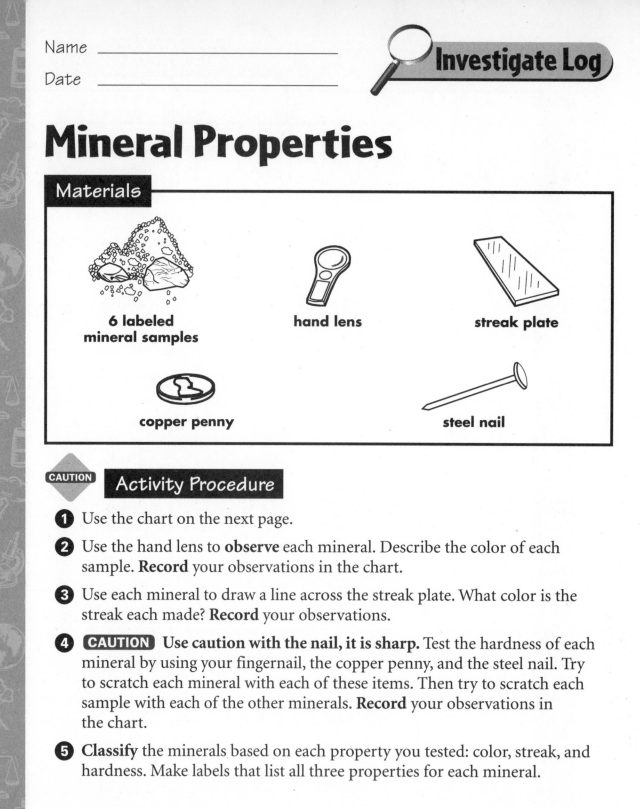

6 labeled mineral samples

hand lens

streak plate

copper penny

steel nail

## CAUTION Activity Procedure

1. Use the chart on the next page.

2. Use the hand lens to **observe** each mineral. Describe the color of each sample. **Record** your observations in the chart.

3. Use each mineral to draw a line across the streak plate. What color is the streak each made? **Record** your observations.

4. **CAUTION** **Use caution with the nail, it is sharp.** Test the hardness of each mineral by using your fingernail, the copper penny, and the steel nail. Try to scratch each mineral with each of these items. Then try to scratch each sample with each of the other minerals. **Record** your observations in the chart.

5. **Classify** the minerals based on each property you tested: color, streak, and hardness. Make labels that list all three properties for each mineral.

Harcourt

| Mineral Sample | Color of the Mineral Sample | Color of the Mineral's Streak | Things that Scratch the Mineral |
|---|---|---|---|
| A | | | |
| B | | | |
| C | | | |
| D | | | |
| E | | | |
| F | | | |

## Draw Conclusions

1. How are the minerals you tested different from each other?

_____

2. Which of the minerals you tested is the hardest? Explain your choice.

_____

_____

3. **Scientists at Work** Scientists **classify** things so it is easier to study them. How

do you think scientists classify minerals? _____

_____

_____

**Investigate Further** Obtain five other unknown mineral samples. Determine the hardness, color, and streak of each. **Classify** all of the mineral samples after testing

the new samples. _____

_____

Harcourt

Name _____

Date _____

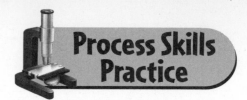

# Classify

When you classify things, you put them into groups based on how they are alike. One way to classify minerals is to group them with other minerals that have similar properties, such as color.

## Think About Classifying

After Ling had finished doing a streak test for several minerals, his teacher gave him a chart that listed different properties of other minerals. He compared each mineral and saw that some of them had similar properties. He also noticed that some of the minerals did not have similar properties.

| Name of the Mineral | How Common the Mineral Is | How Hard the Mineral Is |
|---|---|---|
| Silver | Very rare | Fairly soft |
| Borax | Rare | Soft |
| Quartz | Very common | Hard |
| Diamond | Very rare | Extremely hard |
| Sulfur | Rare | Soft |
| Galena | Very common | Soft |
| Salt (halite) | Very common | Soft |
| Turquoise | Rare | Very hard |

1. How could Ling classify the minerals in the chart? _____

_____

2. Ling has a piece of turquoise. Which of these minerals would scratch the turquoise? Which minerals could the turquoise scratch? Explain.

_____

_____

_____

3. If you had to choose some of these minerals to sell to a rock shop, which ones would you choose and why? _____

_____

_____

**Use with page C33.**

Harcourt

Name _____

Date _____

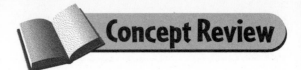

# What Are Minerals?

## Lesson Concept

Minerals are Earth's materials that have never been alive. They may be formed in the mantle or the crust.

## Vocabulary

**mineral** (C34)    **streak** (C35)    **luster** (C35)    **hardness** (C35)

**Answer the questions about minerals below.**

**1.** Where and how do minerals form? Give three different examples.

_____

_____

_____

_____

**2.** Define three different properties of minerals, and give examples of each one.

_____

_____

_____

_____

**3.** In the space below, draw a picture of the kitchen in your home. Point out four different uses of minerals there.

Harcourt

**Use with page C37.**

# Identifying Rocks

## Materials

**5 labeled rock samples**

**hand lens**

**dropper**

**safety goggles**

**vinegar**

**paper plate**

**paper towels**

## Activity Procedure

**CAUTION**

1. Use the chart on the next page.

2. Use the hand lens to **observe** each rock. What color or colors is each rock? **Record** your observations in your chart.

3. Can you see any grains, or small pieces, making up the rock? Are the grains very small, or are they large? Are they rounded, or do they have sharp edges? Do the grains fit together like puzzle pieces? Or are they just next to one another? **Record** your observations under *Texture* in your chart. Draw a picture of each rock in the *Picture* column.

4. **CAUTION** **Put on your safety goggles.** Vinegar bubbles when it is dropped on the mineral calcite. Put the rock samples on the paper plate. Use the dropper to put a few drops of vinegar on each rock. **Observe** what happens. **Record** your findings.

5. **Classify** your rocks into two groups based on how the rocks are alike.

Harcourt

Name _____

| Rock Sample | Color | Texture | Picture | Bubbles When Vinegar Added |
|-------------|-------|---------|---------|----------------------------|
| 1 | | | | |
| 2 | | | | |
| 3 | | | | |
| 4 | | | | |
| 5 | | | | |

## Draw Conclusions

1. What properties did you use to **classify** your rocks? _____

_____

2. How does your classification system **compare** with those of two other students?

_____

_____

3. **Scientists at Work** One way scientists **classify** rocks is by how they formed. Choose one rock and explain how you think it might have formed.

_____

_____

**Investigate Further** Take a walk around your school or neighborhood. Using your **observations**, list at least three ways people use rocks.

_____

_____

Harcourt

Name _____

Date _____

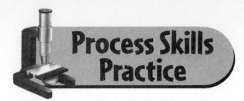

# Classify

When you classify rocks, you put them into groups based on how the rocks are alike.

## Think About Classifying

Malcom's teacher gave him a picture of four rocks, like the ones shown below. Malcom classified the rocks based on what they look like. Then he made a chart showing his classification.

**A**

**B**

**C**

**D**

| Characteristic Used for Classifying | Rocks in the Group |
|---|---|
| Presence of pores | A and C |
| Presence of cracks | B and D |

1. Malcom based his classification on the types of breaks in the rocks. What other features could he use to classify these rocks? _____

_____

2. What tests could he do to help classify the rocks? _____

_____

_____

3. Gabbro is a kind of rock made up of a few light-colored minerals sprinkled in with mostly dark-colored minerals. Basalt is a kind of rock made up of tiny pieces of these same types of minerals. Which rocks in the picture would you classify as gabbro? Which would you classify as basalt? Explain your reasoning

for each decision. _____

_____

_____

Harcourt

Name _____

Date _____

# What Are Rocks?

Rocks are made up of one or more minerals. They are classified as igneous, sedimentary, or metamorphic.

## Vocabulary

**rock** (C40)        **igneous rock** (C40)        **weathering** (C42)

**erosion** (C42)        **sedimentary rock** (C42)        **metamorphic rock** (C44)

**Fill in the missing parts of the chart. Some blanks will need more than one word.**

| Type of Rock | How Rock Forms | Examples |
|---|---|---|
| _____ _____ | From melted rock that hardens | _____: made of feldspar and pyroxene in hardening lava. |
| | | _____: made of feldspar, quartz, and mica in cooling _____. |
| Sedimentary rock | _____ _____ _____ | Conglomerate: made of _____ _____ as big as _____ or as small as peas. |
| | | _____: made of calcite, sometimes from seashells. |
| | | Shale: Made of sediments that are very _____. |
| _____ _____ | From rock that has undergone great heat and pressure | Marble: Formed from _____ that was squeezed and heated. |
| | | _____: Formed from shale exposed to great pressure. |

# The Rock Cycle

## Materials

3 pieces of modeling clay,
each a different color

small objects—pieces of aquarium
gravel, fake jewels, and a
few pennies

2 aluminum pie pans

## Activity Procedure

**1** The small objects stand for minerals. Press the "minerals" into the three pieces of clay. Each color of clay with its objects stands for a different igneous rock.

**2** Now suppose that wind and water are weathering and eroding the "rocks." To **model** this process, break one rock into pieces (sediments) and drop the pieces into one of the pie pans (a lake).

**3** Drop pieces from the second rock on top of the first rock layer. Then drop pieces of the third rock on top of the second layer. Press the layers together by using the bottom of the empty pie pan. What kind of rock have you made?

**4** Squeeze the "sedimentary rock" between your hands to warm it up. What causes the rock to change? Which kind of rock is it now?

Harcourt

**Investigate Log**

## Draw Conclusions

**1.** How did the igneous "rocks" change in this investigation ? _____

_____

_____

_____

_____

**2.** What might weathering and erosion do to a metamorphic rock?

_____

_____

_____

**3.** **Scientists at Work** Scientists often **make a model** to help them understand processes that occur in nature. What process did your hands represent in

Step 4 of the activity? _____

_____

_____

_____

**Investigate Further** Tell how you could change this model to show igneous rocks that formed from magma and igneous rocks that formed from lava.

_____

_____

_____

_____

_____

Harcourt

Name _____

Date _____

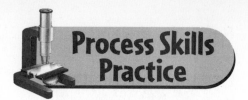

# Make a Model

Making a model can help you understand processes that are hard to observe because they occur over a very long time in nature.

## Think About Making a Model

Gabe read about sedimentary rocks forming from pieces of rock dropped by moving water. He read that small sediments are carried farther and are dropped later than larger sediments are. He made a model to try to see how this worked.

Gabe put small pebbles, coarse sand, and mud in a large jar and filled the jar with water. He shook the jar for several minutes, until the water was cloudy and gray. Then he set the jar on a table. He started observing the jar ten minutes later and continued making observations every five minutes for the next twenty-five minutes.

| Number of Minutes | Height of the Sediment | Observations |
|---|---|---|
| 10 | 4 centimeters | The water is very cloudy, and pebbles have all settled to the bottom of the jar. |
| 15 | 5 centimeters | The sediment layer is still cloudy. |
| 20 | 7 centimeters | The sand is beginning to settle on the bottom of the jar. |
| 25 | 10 centimeters | The sand has settled some more, but the clay particles are still floating in the water. |

1. Based on what he had read, what do you think Gabe expected would happen with his model? _____

_____

2. Did Gabe's model show what he was interested in learning about? Explain.

_____

_____

3 How is Gabe's model not like a river? _____

_____

Harcourt

# What Is the Rock Cycle?

## Lesson Concept

Rocks change from one kind to another in the rock cycle.

## Vocabulary

**rock cycle** (C50)

**Complete the captions for each of the pictures below to describe parts of the rock cycle.**

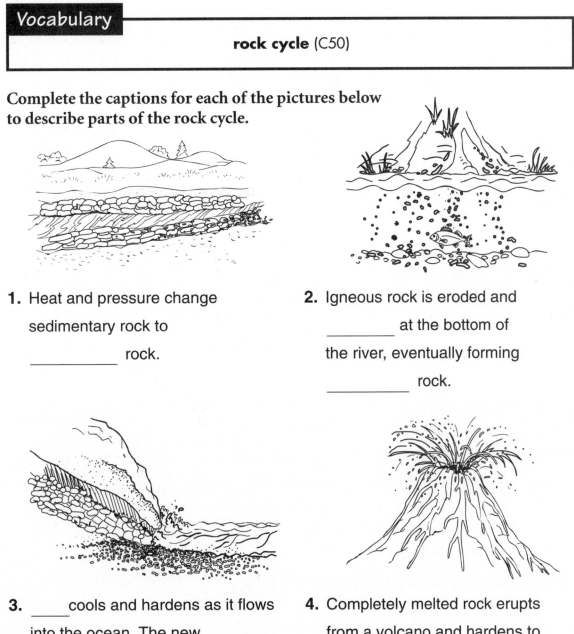

**1.** Heat and pressure change sedimentary rock to _____ rock.

**2.** Igneous rock is eroded and _____ at the bottom of the river, eventually forming _____ rock.

**3.** _____ cools and hardens as it flows into the ocean. The new _____ rock is weathered and eroded by waves.

**4.** Completely melted rock erupts from a volcano and hardens to form _____ rock.

# Recognize Vocabulary

Write the letter of the best answer on the line.

| mineral | streak | hardness | luster |
|---------|--------|----------|--------|
| rock | sedimentary rock | igneous rock | metamorphic rock |
| erosion | weathering | rock cycle | |

_____ 1. a solid material, formed in nature, with particles arranged in a repeated pattern

_____ 2. the breaking down of rocks by wind, water, ice, and plant roots

_____ 3. a material made up of one or more minerals

_____ 4. the way the surface of a mineral reflects light

_____ 5. the movement of weathered rock pieces from one place to another

_____ 6. rocks that form when melted rock hardens

_____ 7. the color of powder left behind when you rub a mineral against a white tile

_____ 8. rocks that have been changed by high heat or very high pressure

_____ 9. the changes rocks go through as they change back and forth from igneous to sedimentary to metamorphic rock

_____ 10. rocks that form when layers of rock particles are squeezed or stuck together

_____ 11. a mineral's ability to resist being scratched

**A** erosion

**B** hardness

**C** igneous rocks

**D** luster

**E** metamorphic rocks

**F** mineral

**G** rock

**H** rock cycle

**I** sedimentary rocks

**J** streak

**K** weathering

**Use with pages C32–C51.**

# Chapter 3 • Graphic Organizer for Chapter Concepts

## Fossils

### LESSON 1
### FOSSIL FORMATION

How Fossils Form

1. _____

2. _____

Types of Trace Fossils

1. _____

2. _____

3. _____

4. _____

5. _____

Other Fossil Types

1. _____

2. _____

3. _____

4. _____

5. _____

### LESSON 2
### WHAT FOSSILS TELL US

How Living Things Have Changed

1. _____

2. _____

3. _____

Importance of Fossils

1. _____

2. _____

3. _____

# Making a Fossil

## Materials

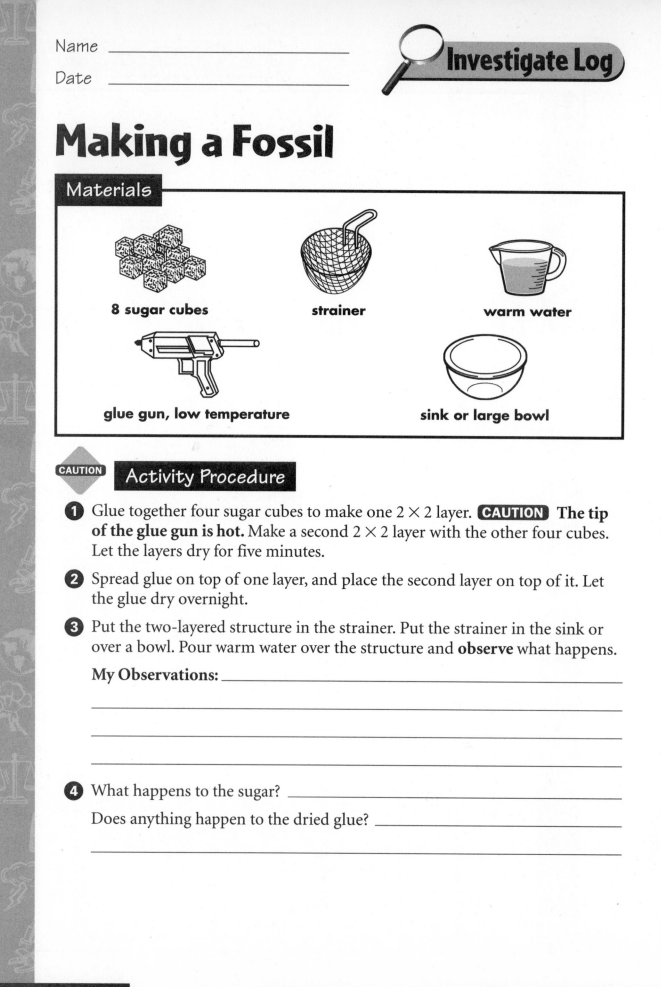

8 sugar cubes

strainer

warm water

glue gun, low temperature

sink or large bowl

**CAUTION** ## Activity Procedure

1. Glue together four sugar cubes to make one 2 × 2 layer. **CAUTION** **The tip of the glue gun is hot.** Make a second 2 × 2 layer with the other four cubes. Let the layers dry for five minutes.

2. Spread glue on top of one layer, and place the second layer on top of it. Let the glue dry overnight.

3. Put the two-layered structure in the strainer. Put the strainer in the sink or over a bowl. Pour warm water over the structure and **observe** what happens.

**My Observations:** _____

_____

_____

_____

4. What happens to the sugar? _____

Does anything happen to the dried glue? _____

_____

Harcourt

Name _____

## Draw Conclusions

1. In your model what parts of a plant or an animal did the sugar cubes

   stand for? _____

   What parts of a plant or an animal did the dried glue stand for?

   _____

   _____

2. In your model, what process did the warm water stand for? _____

   _____

   _____

3. **Scientists at Work** Scientists often **make inferences** based on their
   observations. What can you infer about how fossils form, based on

   what you learned in the investigation? _____

   _____

   _____

   **Investigate Further** With an adult's permission, bury a cooked chicken leg
   about 15 cm deep in the ground outdoors. After a couple of weeks, put on rubber
   gloves and goggles and dig up the chicken leg. **Observe** how it has changed.
   What happened to the soft parts of the chicken leg? Did the hard parts change?

   _____

   _____

   _____

   _____

   _____

   _____

Harcourt

Name _____

Date _____

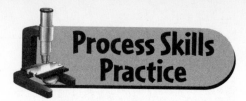

# Infer

When you infer, you use knowledge or information you already have to explain something you can observe. You can infer that if you glue two sheets of paper together, they will stick together. You know this because you know glue is sticky.

## Think About Inferring

When organisms die, they usually decay quickly and disappear without leaving a trace. Sometimes, however, all or part of an organism gets preserved in rock. The preserved remains of organisms are called fossils.

1. What kind of rock do you infer would be most likely to contain fossils?

   **A** igneous rock       **B** metamorphic rock       **C** sedimentary rock

2. What knowledge and observations did you use to make your inference?

   _____

   _____

   _____

3. In which of the following places would you infer fossil-bearing rocks are most likely to form?

   **A** in a forest       **B** in a volcano       **C** under a glacier   **D** under the ocean

4. What knowledge and observations did you use to make your inference?

   _____

   _____

   _____

5. If you were going on a trip to collect fossils, which tools do you think would be most useful to bring along?

   **A** a hand lens       **B** a hammer       **C** a microscope       **D** a computer

6. What knowledge and observations did you use to make your inference?

   _____

   _____

   _____

Harcourt

**Use with page C61.**

# How Do Fossils Form?

Fossils are the remains of living things that lived on Earth long ago.

**Vocabulary**

**fossil** (C62)    **trace fossil** (C63)    **mold** (C64)    **cast** (C64)

**Answer the questions below about fossils.**

1. A crab shell is buried in sediments. The sediments get pressed and squeezed into stone. Meanwhile, the crab shell gets washed away, leaving a hollow space the shape of the crab shell. What kind of fossil is this? _____

2. An insect is trapped in the sap of an evergreen tree. The tree sap hardens to form a clear, yellow material. The entire body of the insect is preserved. What is the material that holds the fossil called? _____

3. A leaf is buried in sediments. The sediments are exposed to high heat and pressure. As this happens, most of the chemicals in the leaf evaporate. The only thing that remains is a thin, black film that is in the shape of the leaf. What is this kind of fossil called? _____

4. A tree trunk is buried in sediments. Minerals slowly take the place of the materials that formed the tree trunk. Even the structures of the cells are preserved. What do we call a fossil that forms in this way?

_____

5. Fossil footprints of an extinct kind of elephant are preserved in rock. Tracks a snake made in sand are preserved in another kind of rock. What do we call these kinds of fossils? _____

6. A hollow space was left where a bone belonging to an ancient bird had been buried. Minerals filled in the hollow space. What do we call a fossil that forms this way? _____

# Sets of Animal Tracks

## Materials

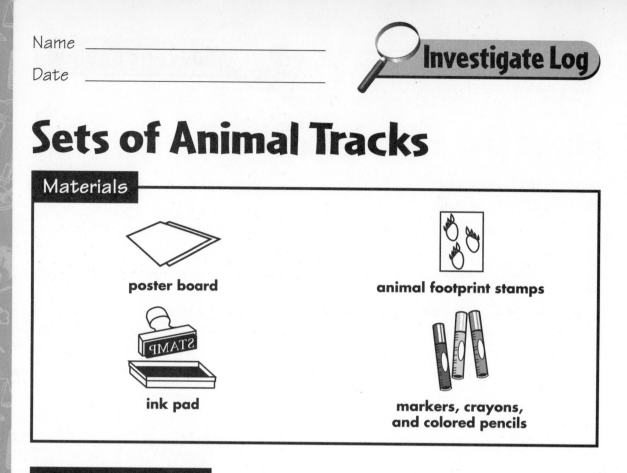

poster board

animal footprint stamps

ink pad

markers, crayons, and colored pencils

## Activity Procedure

**1** On the poster board, draw a picture of an area where animal tracks are found. The picture might show a riverbank or a sandy beach.

**2** Each person in your group should choose a different animal. Mark these animals' tracks on the poster board. Use the ink pad and stamps, or any of the other items. Make sure that some sets of tracks go over other sets. Keep a record of which animal made tracks first, second, third, and so on.

**3** When your group has finished making tracks, trade poster boards with another group. Try to figure out the order in which the other group's tracks were made. **Record** your conclusions in an ordered list. Give reasons for the order you chose. **Compare** your conclusions with the written record of the other group's track order.

**My conclusions:** _____

_____

_____

Harcourt

Name _____

## Draw Conclusions

1. Did all the animals move in the same way? If not, how could you tell the kind of animal from the tracks it made? _____

_____

_____

_____

2. How did your group decide which tracks were made first?

_____

_____

_____

_____

3. **Scientists at Work** Scientists can **infer** relationships among rock layers and the fossils they contain. They do this after carefully **observing** the rocks and fossils. What observations led you to infer the order in which the footprints were

made? _____

_____

**Investigate Further** Get a potato. Using a plastic knife, carefully carve the potato into an animal track stamp. Use an ink pad and the stamp to make some tracks on a sheet of paper. Have a classmate **infer** from the tracks how the "animal" moves. Does it slither? Does it walk on two legs or four legs? Or does the animal

jump or fly to get from place to place? _____

_____

_____

_____

Harcourt

# Observe and Infer

Observing involves examining objects carefully. Inferring involves using those observations to come up with an explanation about something related to the objects.

## Think About Observing and Inferring

Tamara learns that scientists have found many fossil skeletons of ocean-dwelling reptiles called plesiosaurs (plee•see•uh•SAHRZ). These animals have bones similar to those of other reptiles. Scientists are not sure what the plesiosaurs preyed on. They found a fossil plesiosaur with the remains of many fossil shellfish in the place where the plesiosaur's stomach may have been. The plesiosaur might have eaten these shellfish.

Tamara observes a picture of a plesiosaur. She sees that it has flippers and swims in the oceans. She notes that its jawbone is long and narrow. The jawbone has many long, sharp teeth.

1. On the chart below, list the observations and inferences Tamara made. The inferences may be stated or implied.

| Observations | Inferences |
|---|---|
|  |  |
|  |  |
|  |  |
|  |  |

2. What are some other possible inferences Tamara could have made about the shellfish found with the plesiosaurs? _____

_____

_____

Harcourt

Name _____

Date _____

# What Can We Learn from Fossils?

Fossils tell us about living things of the past, how living things have changed over time, and how Earth has changed.

**Answer the questions below.**

1. How can scientists use the order of rock layers to learn about the ages of

   different rocks? _____

2. Scientists study rock layers. What evidence do they gather from their studies?

   _____

   _____

3. Name and describe two living things that have changed over time.

   _____

   _____

   _____

   _____

4. Give an example of an animal that has changed over the span of geologic time.
   Tell how scientists know about these changes. What do these changes also tell

   about how Earth has changed over time? _____

   _____

   _____

   _____

Harcourt

# Recognize Vocabulary

**Read the paragraph below. Then use the vocabulary terms from the terms below to fill in the blanks in Dad's letter to Bob and Maria.**

| fossil | trace fossil | mold | cast |
|---|---|---|---|

A hardworking geologist has just discovered an area rich in fossils that no one has ever seen before. He wants to send a letter to his family to tell them about his discovery. Here is the first draft of his letter. Help him edit the letter by filling in the blanks with the vocabulary terms that match the definition of the boldfaced terms, which may be difficult for his young children to understand.

Dear Bob and Maria,

    I had the best day of my life today! I went for a hike in a dusty valley. In the spring, when the snow in the nearby mountains melts, water rushes through this valley. But now it is completely dry. I kept my eyes open for

**(remains or traces of once-living things in rock)** _____
in the bare cliffs. I saw some bones sticking out from the side of a rock. I recognized them. They formed the skeleton of a fish. I stopped and looked more closely. In the same rocks I saw **(fossils made up of imprints left by**

**the outside of a dead plant or animal)** _____ of some
shells. Above me in a layer of rock that was a different color, I saw a
**(fossil that formed when sediments filled in a fossil mold)**

_____ of a pine cone. In that same layer, I saw a
**(fossil that showed changes once-living animals made in their**

**surroundings)** _____ of what looked like very large
droppings!

Love,
Dad

Harcourt

# Chapter 1 • Graphic Organizer for Chapter Concepts

## Weather Conditions

### LESSON 1
### EARTH'S ATMOSPHERE

Describe the Atmosphere

1. _____

2. _____

Four Layers of the Atmosphere

3. _____

4. _____

5. _____

6. _____

### LESSON 2
### AIR MASSES AFFECT WEATHER

Describe an Air Mass

1. _____

2. _____

3. _____

Fronts

4. form _____

5. cold front _____

6. warm front _____

### LESSON 3
### WEATHER PREDICTION

Weather Conditions and the Instruments Used to Measure Them

1. _____

2. _____

3. _____

4. _____

5. _____

Weather Maps

6. _____

7. _____

Harcourt

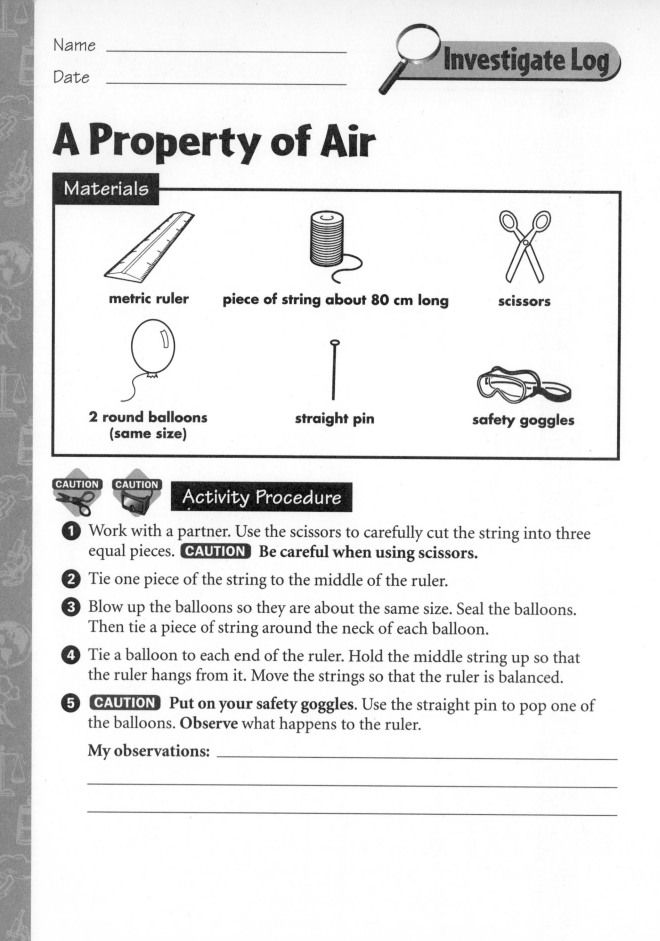
# A Property of Air

## Materials

metric ruler

piece of string about 80 cm long

scissors

2 round balloons
(same size)

straight pin

safety goggles

**CAUTION** **CAUTION** ### Activity Procedure

**1** Work with a partner. Use the scissors to carefully cut the string into three equal pieces. **CAUTION** **Be careful when using scissors.**

**2** Tie one piece of the string to the middle of the ruler.

**3** Blow up the balloons so they are about the same size. Seal the balloons. Then tie a piece of string around the neck of each balloon.

**4** Tie a balloon to each end of the ruler. Hold the middle string up so that the ruler hangs from it. Move the strings so that the ruler is balanced.

**5** **CAUTION** **Put on your safety goggles.** Use the straight pin to pop one of the balloons. **Observe** what happens to the ruler.

**My observations:** _____

_____

_____

Harcourt

Name _____

## Draw Conclusions

1. Explain how this investigation shows that air takes up space.

_____

_____

2. Describe what happened when one balloon was popped. What property
of air caused what you **observed**? _____

_____

_____

3. **Scientists at Work** Scientists often **infer** conclusions when the answer to
a question is not clear or can't be **observed** directly. Your breath is invisible, but
you observed how it made the balloons and the ruler behave. Even though you
can't see air, what can you infer about whether or not air is matter? Explain.

_____

_____

_____

_____

**Investigate Further** The air around you presses on you and everything else on
Earth. This property of air, called air pressure, is a result of air's weight. When
more air is packed into a small space, air pressure increases. You can feel air
pressure for yourself. Hold your hands around a partly filled balloon while your
partner blows it up. Describe what happens. Then **infer** which property of air

helps keep the tires of a car inflated. _____

_____

_____

_____

Harcourt

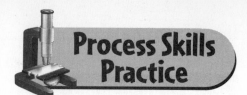

# Observe and Infer

You make observations when you notice details. You make inferences when you use those details to come up with a possible explanation for why or how an event occurred.

## Think About Observing and Inferring

Martha crumpled several pieces of paper and stuffed them into the bottom of a drinking glass. She pushed the glass straight down into a bowl of water. She held the glass down for one minute. During that minute nothing happened. The paper stayed where it was in the glass, and no bubbles rose to the surface of the water. Then Martha pulled the glass straight out of the water. She pulled the paper out of the bottom of the drinking glass. The paper and the inside of the glass were dry.

**1.** Fill in the table below with observations Martha made.

| When Observation Was Made | Observation |
|---|---|
| Before the experiment | |
| During the experiment | |
| During the experiment | |
| After the experiment | |

**2.** What inferences might Martha make from her observations? _____

_____

_____

_____

_____

_____

Harcourt

Name _____

Date _____

# What Makes Up Earth's Atmosphere?

## Lesson Concept

Earth is surrounded by four thin layers of air called the atmosphere.

## Vocabulary

**atmosphere** (D6)   **air pressure** (D7)   **troposphere** (D8)   **stratosphere** (D8)

**Answer the questions below.**

**1.** Describe how the atmosphere formed and changed over time. _____

_____

_____

_____

**2.** What does carbon dioxide in the atmosphere do? _____

_____

**Label the diagram of the atmosphere, and describe each layer. In your descriptions, tell where the air pressure is highest and where it is lowest, where the temperature is highest and lowest, and where the ozone layer is.**

**3.** Layer: _____

Description: _____

_____

**4.** Layer: _____

Description: _____

_____

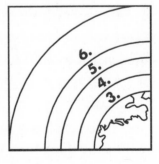

**5.** Layer: _____

Description: _____

_____

_____

**6.** Layer: _____

Description: _____

_____

_____

Harcourt

**Use with page D9.**

# Wind Speed

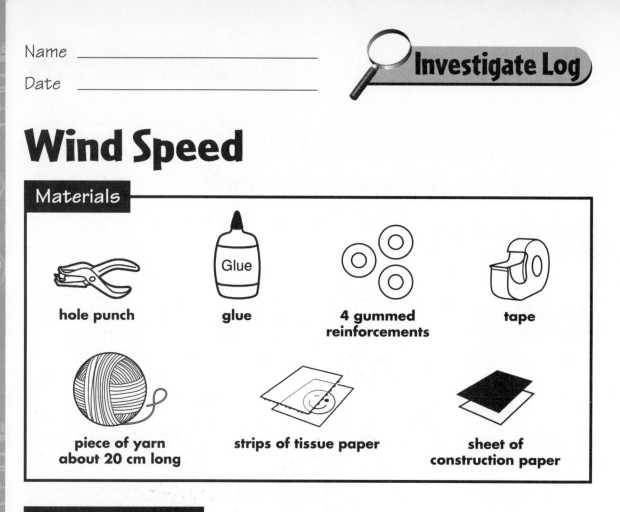

hole punch  glue  4 gummed reinforcements  tape

piece of yarn about 20 cm long  strips of tissue paper  sheet of construction paper

## Activity Procedure

**1** Form a cylinder with the sheet of construction paper. Tape the edge of the paper to keep the cylinder from opening.

**2** Use the hole punch to make two holes at one end of the cylinder. Punch them on opposite sides of the cylinder and about 3 cm from the end. Put two gummed reinforcements on each hole, one on the inside and one on the outside.

**3** Thread the yarn through the holes, and tie it tightly to form a handle loop.

**4** Glue strips of tissue paper to the other end of the cylinder. Put tape over the glued strips to hold them better. Your completed windsock should look like the one shown in Picture B on page D11 of your textbook.

**5** Hang your windsock outside. Use the chart on the next page to **measure** wind speed each day for several days. **Record** your measurements in a chart. Include the date, time of day, observations of objects affected by the wind, and the approximate wind speed.

Harcourt

Name _____

| Wind Scale | | | |
|---|---|---|---|
| **Speed in km/hr** | **Description** | **Observations on Land** | **Windsock Position** |
| 0 | no breeze | no movement of wind | limp |
| 6–19 | light breeze | leaves rustle, wind vanes move, wind felt on face | slightly up |
| 20–38 | moderate breeze | dust and paper blow, small branches sway | nearly 90 degrees to arm |
| 39–49 | strong breeze | umbrellas hard to open, large branches sway | stiff and 90 degrees from arm |

## Draw Conclusions

1. How fast was the weakest wind you **measured**? _____

    _____

    How fast was the strongest wind? _____

2. How did you determine the speed of the wind? _____

    _____

    _____

3. **Scientists at Work** *Light, moderate,* and *strong* are adjectives describing wind speed. Scientists often use number **measurements** to describe things because, in science, numbers are more exact than words. What is the wind speed **measurement**, in kilometers per hour, if the wind is making large tree branches sway? _____

**Investigate Further** Use a magnetic compass to determine which way is north from your windsock. **Measure** both wind speed and direction each day for a week. **Record** your data in a chart.

Harcourt

Name _____

Date _____

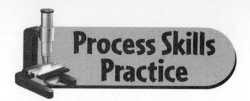

# Measure

Reading measurements allows you to communicate precise information about an event.

## Think About Measuring

Hurricanes are powerful storms that form near the equator over warm ocean water that is at least 27°C (81°F). In the Northern Hemisphere, hurricane winds blow in a counterclockwise direction. In the Southern Hemisphere, hurricane winds blow in a clockwise direction. To be classified as a hurricane, the winds must blow at least 119 km/hr. A hurricane swirls around an area of low air pressure. The eye of the storm is a calm region at the center of the hurricane that has the lowest air pressure and generally the highest air temperatures.

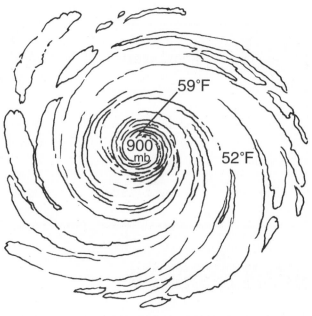

1. Normal air pressure is 985 millibars. What is the difference (in millibars) between the air pressure in the eye of the storm and normal air pressure?

_____

2. What is the temperature difference between the eye of the storm and the main

   body of the storm? _____

3. Imagine the storm is traveling toward a coastal city 100 kilometers away at 15 km/hr. How long would it take the storm to reach the city? Show how you figured this out.

_____

4. Which hemisphere could this storm form in? Explain your answer.

_____

_____

Harcourt

Use with page D11.

# How Do Air Masses Affect Weather?

## Lesson Concept

The sun warms Earth unevenly, forming air masses of different temperatures.

## Vocabulary

**greenhouse effect** (D12)          **air mass** (D13)          **front** (D14)

**Fill in the blanks below by describing what happens to the sun's radiation.**

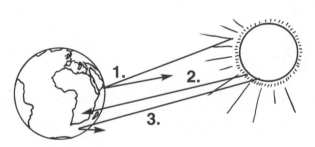

1. _____

2. _____

3. _____

**Label the key for the weather map.**

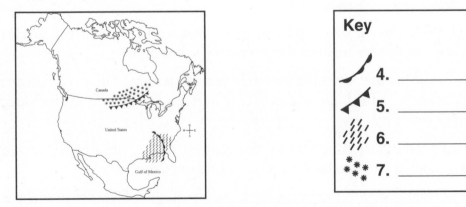

**Key**

4. _____

5. _____

6. _____

7. _____

**8.** Describe a warm front, and tell what happens as a warm front moves through

an area. _____

_____

_____

_____

# Air Pressure

## Materials

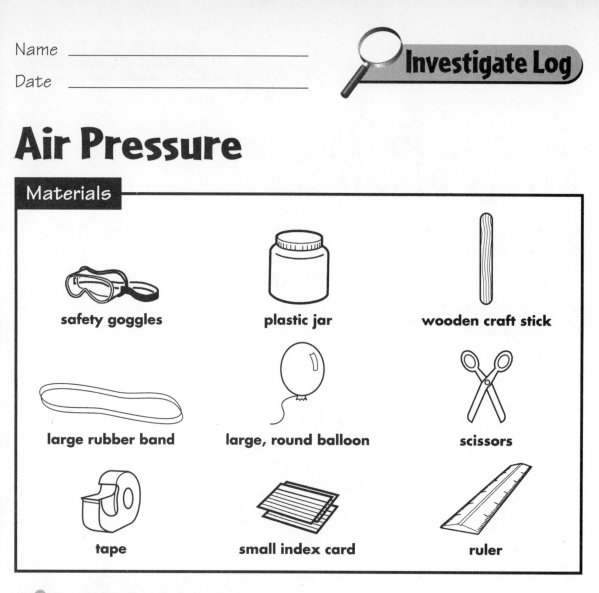

safety goggles     plastic jar     wooden craft stick

large rubber band     large, round balloon     scissors

tape     small index card     ruler

## Activity Procedure

1. **CAUTION** **Put on your safety goggles. Be careful when using scissors.** Use the scissors to carefully cut the neck off the balloon.

2. Have your partner hold the jar while you stretch the balloon over the open end. Make sure the balloon fits snugly over the jar. Secure the balloon with the rubber band.

3. Tape the craft stick to the top of the balloon. Make sure that more than half of the craft stick stretches out from the edge of the jar.

4. On the blank side of the index card, use a pencil and a ruler to make a thin line. Label the line *Day 1*. Tape the card to a wall. Make sure the line is at the same height as the wooden stick on your barometer.

5. At the same time each day for a week, **measure** relative air pressure by marking the position of the wooden stick on the index card. Write the correct day next to each reading.

Harcourt

## Investigate Log

### Draw Conclusions

**1.** Describe how air pressure changed during the time that you were **measuring** it. _____

_____

**2.** What might have caused your barometer to show little or no change during the time you were taking **measurements**? _____

_____

_____

**3.** **Scientists at Work** Meteorologists are scientists who use instruments to **measure** weather data. How did your barometer measure air pressure?

_____

_____

_____

**Investigate Further** Use your air pressure **measurements** and information from daily weather reports to **predict** the weather in your area for the next few days.

_____

_____

_____

_____

Harcourt

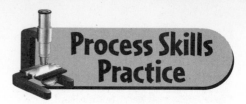

# Measure

By measuring carefully, you can learn how weather conditions change from day to day.

## Think About Measuring

Read the barometers below, and record the measurements of air pressure. Then answer the question.

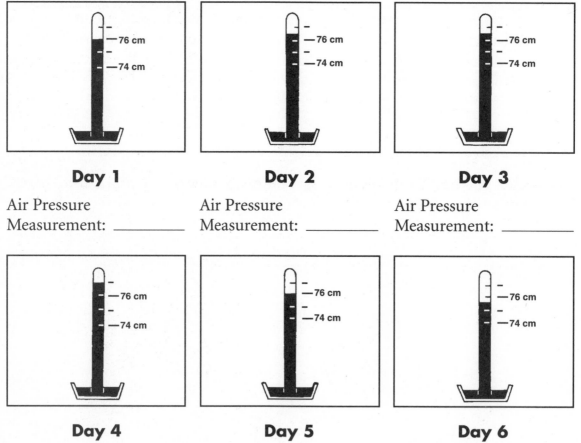

**Day 1**

Air Pressure
Measurement: _____

**Day 2**

Air Pressure
Measurement: _____

**Day 3**

Air Pressure
Measurement: _____

**Day 4**

Air Pressure
Measurement: _____

**Day 5**

Air Pressure
Measurement: _____

**Day 6**

Air Pressure
Measurement: _____

**1.** Air pressure at sea level is at its average when it reads 76 cm (29.5 in.) on the mercury barometer. On which days is a high pressure system moving through?

When might a front, bringing low pressure be on its way? _____

_____

_____

Harcourt

Name _____

Date _____

# How Is Weather Predicted?

## Lesson Concept

Meteorologists use many kinds of tools to help them predict weather.

## Vocabulary

**barometer** (D20)     **humidity** (D21)     **anemometer** (D21)

**Read each statement, and decide whether it is true or false. On the line, write** *True* **if the statement is true or** *False* **if the statement is false.**

_____ **1.** You can measure air pressure with a thermometer.

_____ **2.** Most cold air masses have higher air pressure than most warm air masses.

_____ **3.** The amount of moisture in the air is called humidity.

_____ **4.** Cool air holds more moisture than warm air does.

_____ **5.** Meteorologists measure wind speed using a barometer.

**Use the weather map to answer the questions.**

**6.** What states shown have a warm front? _____

**7.** What states shown have a cold front? _____

**8.** What states shown have rain? _____

**9.** If you were a meteorologist, what kind of weather would you predict Santa Fe, New Mexico will have tomorrow? Little Rock, Arkansas? _____

_____

**Use with page D23.**

Harcourt

**Workbook** WB153

# Recognize Vocabulary

| | | |
|---|---|---|
| atmosphere | air pressure | troposphere |
| stratosphere | greenhouse effect | air mass |
| front | barometer | humidity |
| anemometer | | |

For each pair of terms, write how they are the same and different in meaning.

**1.** stratosphere and troposphere

_____

_____

_____

**2.** air mass and front

_____

_____

_____

**3.** barometer and anemometer

_____

_____

_____

Match each term in Column A with its meaning in Column B.

**Column A**

_____ **4.** humidity

_____ **5.** greenhouse effect

_____ **6.** atmosphere

_____ **7.** air pressure

**Column B**

**A** pressure caused by air particles pressing down on Earth's surface

**B** amount of water vapor in the air

**C** layers of air surrounding Earth

**D** effect of air trapping heat around Earth

Harcourt

# Chapter 2 • Graphic Organizer for Chapter Concepts

## Water In The Oceans

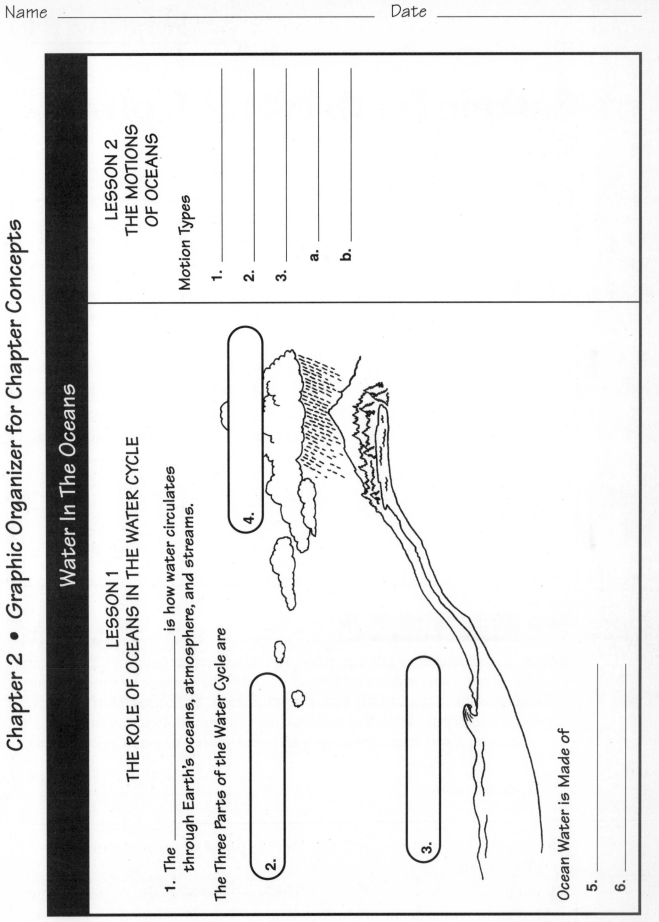

### LESSON 1
### THE ROLE OF OCEANS IN THE WATER CYCLE

1. The _____ is how water circulates through Earth's oceans, atmosphere, and streams.

The Three Parts of the Water Cycle are

2.

3.

4.

Ocean Water is Made of

5. _____

6. _____

### LESSON 2
### THE MOTIONS OF OCEANS

Motion Types

1. _____

2. _____

3. _____

   a. _____

   b. _____

# Getting Fresh Water from Salt Water

## Materials

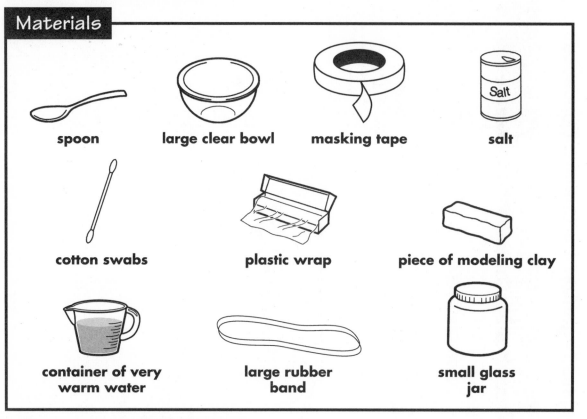

spoon     large clear bowl     masking tape     salt

cotton swabs     plastic wrap     piece of modeling clay

container of very warm water     large rubber band     small glass jar

**CAUTION** **Activity Procedure**

**1** Stir two spoonfuls of salt into the container of very warm water. Put one end of a clean cotton swab into this mixture. Taste the mixture by touching the swab to your tongue. **Record** your **observations.** **CAUTION** **Don't share swabs. Don't put a swab that has touched your mouth back into any substance. Never taste anything in an investigation or experiment unless you are told to do so.**

My observations: _____

_____

**2** Pour the salt water into the large bowl. Put the jar in the center of the bowl of salt water.

**3** Put the plastic wrap over the top of the bowl. The wrap should not touch the top of the jar inside the bowl. Put a large rubber band around the bowl to hold the wrap in place.

Harcourt

**4** Form the clay into a small ball. Put the ball on top of the plastic wrap right over the jar. Make sure the plastic wrap doesn't touch the jar.

**5** On the outside of the bowl, use tape to mark the level of the salt water. Place the bowl in a sunny spot for one day.

**6** After one day, remove the plastic wrap and the clay ball. Use clean swabs to taste the water in the jar and in the bowl. **Record** your **observations**.

**My observations:** _____

_____

## Draw Conclusions

**1.** What did you **observe** by using your sense of taste? _____

_____

_____

**2.** What do you **infer** happened to the salt water as it sat in the sun?

_____

_____

**3. Scientists at Work** The movement of water from the Earth's surface, through the atmosphere, and back to Earth's surface is called the water cycle. From what you **observed,** what can you **infer** about the ocean's role in the water cycle?

_____

_____

_____

**Investigate Further** Put the plastic wrap and the clay back on the large bowl. Leave the bowl in the sun for several days, until all the water in the large bowl is gone. **Observe** the bowl and the jar. What can you **conclude** about ocean water?

_____

_____

_____

_____

Harcourt

Name _____

Date _____

# Observe and Infer

You use your senses to make observations. You use these observations to make inferences, which are explanations or opinions, about what you have observed.

## Think About Observing and Inferring

Eugene wanted to demonstrate to his friends that different bodies of water contain different amounts of salts. He found a table that showed the amount of salt dissolved in the water from lakes and oceans in different parts of the world. He used the table to help mix samples of water with varying salinity. Then he asked his friends to taste his samples and rate them for saltiness.

| Ranking (Least Salty to Most Salty) | Sample |
| --- | --- |
| 1 | E |
| 2 | A |
| 3 | D |
| 4 | F |
| 5 | B |
| 6 | C |

| Body of Water | Salinity | Sample |
| --- | --- | --- |
| Atlantic Ocean | 35 g/1000 g | |
| Arctic Ocean | 31 g/1000 g | |
| Black Sea | 15 g/1000 g | |
| Dead Sea | 300 g/1000 g | |
| Great Salt Lake | 200 g/1000 g | |
| Lake Superior | <1g/1000 g | |

1. The table on the left gives the ranking of the samples by Eugene's friends. Which sample did they rank the most salty? Which sample did they rank the least salty?

   _____

2. The table on the right gives the salinity of different bodies of water. Based on the tables above, infer which of the samples corresponds to which body of water. Then, fill in the right column of the table.

3. Eugene told his friends that they had made an error in their ranking. He said that Sample D was actually saltier than Sample F. Do you think his friends were careless in their work? Explain your answer. _____

   _____

Harcourt

# What Role Do Oceans Play in the Water Cycle?

## Lesson Concept

The interactions between the oceans, other bodies of water, the sun, and the land cause the recycling of most of Earth's water.

## Vocabulary

| | |
|---|---|
| **water cycle** (D34) | **evaporation** (D34) |
| **condensation** (D34) | **precipitation** (D35) |

**Define the following terms, and show where each occurs in the diagram of the water cycle.**

**1.** Evaporation: _____

_____

**2.** Condensation: _____

_____

**3.** Precipitation: _____

_____

_____

**For each of the places listed, say whether the ocean water is saltier than average, of average saltiness, or less salty than average.**

**4.** _____ in the middle of a large ocean

**5.** _____ near the North Pole

**6.** _____ near the equator

**7.** _____ where a river flows into the ocean

Name _____

Date _____

# Water Currents

## Materials

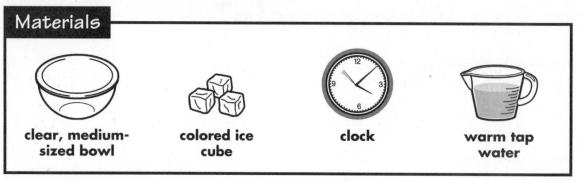

clear, medium-sized bowl

colored ice cube

clock

warm tap water

## Activity Procedure

**1** Put the bowl on a flat surface. Carefully fill the bowl three-quarters full of warm tap water.

**2** Let the water stand undisturbed for 10 minutes.

**3** Without stirring the warm water or making a splash, gently place the colored ice cube in the middle of the bowl.

**4** **Observe** for 10 minutes what happens as the ice cube melts. Every 2 minutes, make a simple drawing of the bowl to **record** your observations.

**My observations:** _____

_____

_____

_____

_____

Harcourt

## Draw Conclusions

**1.** Describe what you **observed** as the ice cube melted in the bowl of warm water.

_____

_____

_____

_____

**2.** In your **model**, what does the bowl of water stand for? _____

_____

What does the ice cube stand for? _____

_____

**3.** Since the liquid in the bowl and the ice cube were both water, what can you **infer** about the cause of what happened in the bowl? _____

_____

_____

_____

**4. Scientists at Work** In Chapter 1, you learned that cold air is denser than warm air. The same is true for water. Using this information and what you **observed** in the investigation, explain one way ocean currents form. _____

_____

_____

_____

**Investigate Further** Mix up two batches of salt water. Use twice as much salt in one batch as in the other. Use the water to **model** another kind of ocean current. Fill a clear bowl three-fourths full with the less salty water. Add a few drops of food coloring to the saltier water. Along the side of the bowl, slowly pour the colored, saltier water into the clear, less salty water. Describe your **observations**. **Make a hypothesis** to explain what you observed. What **prediction** can you make based on the hypothesis? How could you test the prediction? _____

_____

_____

_____

Harcourt

# Observe a Model

You can observe a model to see how salt water mixes with fresh water
and how the water moves in an estuary.

## Think About Observing a Model

David wanted to see if salt water and fresh water mix evenly in an
estuary. He did the following experiment. He filled a bowl half-full of
fresh water. He filled another bowl one-third full of salt water. He put
red food coloring in the salt water and let the two bowls reach room
temperature. Then he slowly poured the salt water into the fresh water,
along the side of the bowl.

1. What was David trying to find out with his model? How did adding food

   coloring to the salt water aid his observations? _____

   _____

   _____

   _____

   _____

2. After David poured the salt water into the fresh water, what do you think he

   focused on observing? _____

   _____

   _____

   _____

3. David watched the bowl of water for a few minutes. He noted that the red-
   colored water sank to the bottom of the bowl and a layer of clear water floated
   on top of the colored layer. Based on David's observations of this model, do
   you think he would expect to find salt water and fresh water evenly mixed in

   an estuary? Explain your answer. _____

   _____

   _____

   _____

Harcourt

Name _____

Date _____

# What Are the Motions of Oceans?

## Lesson Concept

The water in the ocean moves in many different ways.

## Vocabulary

**wave** (D40)          **storm surge** (D41)          **tide** (D42)

**deep ocean current** (D44)          **surface current** (D44)

**Fill in the cause-and-effect chart about ocean movements.**

| Effect | Cause or Causes |
|---|---|
| Waves | |
| Storm surge | |
| Erosion and deposition of sediments along the shore | |
| Daily high and low tides | |
| Spring tides | |
| Neap tides | |
| Surface currents | |
| Deep ocean currents | |

**Use with page D45.**

Harcourt

# Recognize Vocabulary

Fill in the blanks to spell the term defined by the clue. Unscramble the circled letters to make the word, given by the hint at the bottom of the page.

| | | |
|---|---|---|
| water cycle | evaporation | condensation |
| precipitation | wave | storm surge |
| tide | deep ocean current | surface current |

1. up-and-down movement of water particles __ __ __ __

2. water that falls out of the air in the form of rain, snow, sleet, or hail

   __ __ __ __ __ __ __ (__) __ __ __ (__) __ __

3. daily change in the local water level of the ocean __ (__) __ __

4. constant recycling of water on Earth

   __ __ __ __ __ __ (__) __ __

5. a very large wave __ __ __ __ __ __ __ __ __ __

6. process by which a gas changes to a liquid

   __ __ __ __ __ __ __ __ (__) __ __

7. river of water that flows in the ocean that forms because of density differences in ocean water

   __ __ __ __ __ __ __ (__) __ __ __ __ __

8. process by which a liquid changes to a gas

   __ __ (__) __ __ __ __ __ __

9. river of water that flows in the ocean that forms because of a steady wind blowing over the the ocean surface

   __ __ (__) __ __ __ __ __ __ __ __ __

Unscramble the letters to form the name of the world's largest ocean.

The _____ Ocean

# Chapter 3 • Graphic Organizer for Chapter Concepts

## Planets and Other Objects in Space

### LESSON 1
### OBJECTS IN THE SOLAR SYSTEM

The Sun

1. What it is _____ in the center of our solar system.

2. What it is made of _____

3. What it does _____

The Solar System

4. Objects in the solar system _____

How Planets Move

5. _____

6. _____

### LESSON 2
### THE PLANETS

The Inner Planets

1. Surface _____

2. Size _____

3. Names of planets _____

The Outer Planets

4. Surface _____

5. Size _____

6. Moons _____

7. Names of planets _____

Moons and Rings

8. Moons _____

9. Rings _____

### LESSON 3
### PEOPLE STUDY THE SOLAR SYSTEM

1. _____

2. _____

3. _____

### LESSON 4
### CONSTELLATIONS

Constellations

1. What they are _____

How People Use Constellations

2. _____

3. _____

Harcourt

# Planet Movement

## Materials

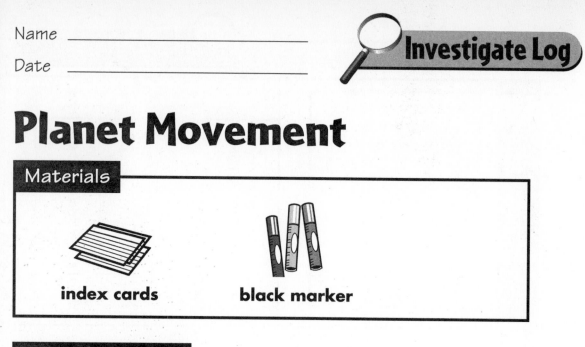

**index cards**          **black marker**

## Activity Procedure

**1** Label one of the cards *Sun*. Label each of the other cards with the name of one of the planets shown in the table on the next page.

**2** Put all of the cards face down on a table and shuffle them. Have each person choose one card.

**3** Use the data table to find out which planet is closest to the sun. Continue **analyzing the data** and **ordering** the cards until you have all the planets in the correct order from the sun.

**4** In the gym or outside on a playground, line up in the order you determined in Step 3.

**5** If you have a planet card, slowly turn around as you walk at a normal pace around the sun. Be sure to stay in your own path. Do not cross paths with other planets. After everyone has gone around the sun once, **record** your **observations** of the planets and their movements.

Harcourt

| Planet | Average Distance from the Sun (millions of km) |
|---|---|
| Earth | 150 |
| Jupiter | 778 |
| Mars | 228 |
| Mercury | 58 |
| Neptune | 4500 |

| Planet | Average Distance from the Sun (millions of km) |
|---|---|
| Pluto | 5900 |
| Saturn | 1429 |
| Uranus | 2871 |
| Venus | 108 |

## Draw Conclusions

1. The sun and the planets that move around it are called the solar system. What is the order of the planets, starting with the one closest to the sun?

   _____

   _____

2. What did you **observe** about the motion of the planets? _____

   _____

   _____

   _____

3. **Scientists at Work** Why did you need to **make a model** to study how planets

   move around the sun? _____

   _____

   _____

   _____

**Investigate Further** Look again at the distances listed in the data table. How could you change your model to make it more accurate? _____

_____

_____

_____

_____

_____

# Make a Model

Making a model can help you understand the motion and interactions of objects in the solar system. These objects are difficult to observe directly because of their large sizes and the vast distances between them.

## Think About Making a Model

Natalie wanted to make a model to see how the phases of the moon formed. She got a flashlight, a basketball, and a baseball. She asked Rodney to help her with the model. She put the flashlight on a table and turned it on. She cleared away the other furniture from the room and turned off the room lights. She stood about 6 feet from the flashlight, holding the basketball at waist height. She asked Rodney to stand a few feet away from her. Rodney held the baseball, just above waist height with his arm straight out in front of him. Rodney slowly walked around her, holding the baseball so the flashlight shined on it.

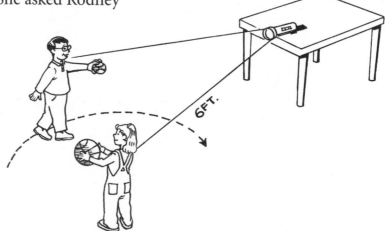

6 FT.

**1.** What did the flashlight represent in Natalie's model? The basketball? The baseball? _____

_____

**2.** What do you think Natalie watched as Rodney walked around her? Why?

_____

_____

**3.** What conclusions could Natalie draw about the phases of the moon by observing her model? Try to list at least two possible conclusions.

_____

_____

_____

Harcourt

Name _____

Date _____

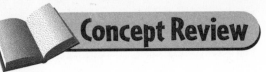

# How Do Objects Move in the Solar System?

## Lesson Concept

The objects in the solar system all revolve around the sun.

## Vocabulary

| | | | |
|---|---|---|---|
| **solar system** (D56) | **star** (D56) | **planet** (D57) | **asteroid** (D57) |
| **comet** (D57) | **orbit** (D58) | **axis** (D58) | |

**Label each of the objects in the solar system.**

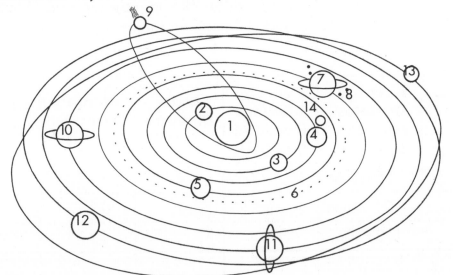

1. _____    8. _____

2. _____    9. _____

3. _____    10. _____

4. _____    11. _____

5. _____    12. _____

6. _____    13. _____

7. _____    14. _____

**Use with page D59.**

# Distances Between Planets

## Materials

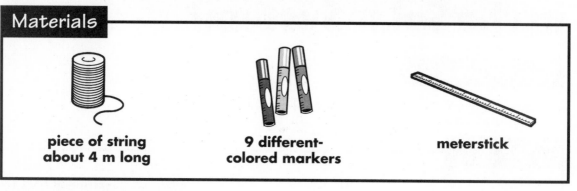

| piece of string about 4 m long | 9 different-colored markers | meterstick |

## Activity Procedure

**1** Use the table below.

**2** At one end of the string, tie three or four knots at the same point to make one large knot. This large knot will stand for the sun in your model.

| Planet | Average Distance from the Sun (km) | Average Distance from the Sun (AU) | Scale Distance (cm) | Planet's Diameter (km) | Marker Color |
|--------|------------------------------------|------------------------------------|---------------------|------------------------|--------------|
| Mercury | 58 million | $\frac{4}{10}$ | 4 | 4876 | |
| Venus | 108 million | $\frac{7}{10}$ | 7 | 12,104 | |
| Earth | 150 million | 1 | | 12,756 | |
| Mars | 228 million | 2 | | 6794 | |
| Jupiter | 778 million | 5 | | 142,984 | |
| Saturn | 1429 million | 10 | | 120,536 | |
| Uranus | 2871 million | 19 | | 51,118 | |
| Neptune | 4500 million | 30 | | 49,532 | |
| Pluto | 5900 million | 39 | | 2274 | |

Harcourt

**3** In the solar system, distances are often measured in astronomical units (AU). One AU equals the average distance from Earth to the sun. In your model, 1 AU will equal 10 cm. Use your meterstick to accurately measure 1 AU from the sun on your model. This point stands for Earth's distance from the sun. Use one of the markers to mark this point on the string. Note in your table which color you used.

**4** Complete the Scale Distance column of the table. Then measure and mark the position of each planet on the string. Use a different color for each planet, and **record** in your table the colors you used.

## Draw Conclusions

1. In your **model**, how far from the sun is Mercury? _____
   How far away is Pluto? _____

2. What advantages can you think of for using AU to measure distances inside the solar system? _____

   _____

   _____

   _____

   _____

3. **Scientists at Work** Explain how it helped to **make a scale model** instead of trying to show actual distances between planets. _____

   _____

   _____

   _____

**Investigate Further** You can use a calculator to help make other scale models. The table gives the actual diameters of the planets. Use this scale: Earth's diameter = 1 cm. Find the scale diameters of the other planets by dividing their actual diameters by Earth's diameter. Make a scale drawing showing the diameter of each planet. _____

_____

_____

_____

_____

Harcourt

Name _____

Date _____

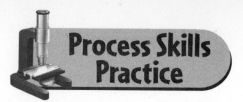

# Make a Model

Making scale models can help you understand size relationships among different objects.

### Think About Making a Model

The table below lists the sizes of some of the different planets and their moons.

| Object | Diameter | Object | Diameter |
|--------|----------|--------|----------|
| Jupiter | 142,800 km | Earth | 12,756 km |
| Ganymede | 5270 km | Moon | 3484 km |
| Europa | 3275 km | Mars | 6794 km |
| Amalthea | 265 km | Deimos | 15 km |
| | | Phobos | 27 km |

1. Compare the diameter of Jupiter with the diameters of its moons. If you were going to make scale models less than 3 meters wide of Jupiter and these three moons, which scale would you choose? Circle your choice.

   **A** 10 km = 1 cm          **B** 100 km = 1 cm          **C** 1000 km = 1 cm

2. Tell how big each object would be using the scale you chose above.

   Jupiter _____        Europa _____

   Ganymede _____        Amalthea _____

3. Would it work to use the same scale you used for Jupiter for making models of

   Mars and its moons? Why or why not? _____

   _____

   _____

4. Pick a scale from Question 1 for making models of Earth and Earth's moon. Write down your scale and the size each of these objects would be.

   Scale _____

   Earth _____

   Moon _____

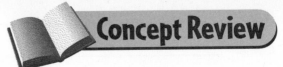
**Concept Review**

# What Are the Planets Like?

## Lesson Concept

Each planet in our solar system is unique.

## Vocabulary

**inner planets** (D62)     **outer planets** (D64)     **gas giants** (D64)

**Answer the questions about the planets.**

**1.** What are three ways Mercury is like Earth's moon? _____

_____

_____

**2.** Compare and contrast Venus with Earth. _____

_____

_____

**3.** Give three facts about the geology of Mars. _____

_____

_____

**4.** How are Jupiter and Saturn alike and different? _____

_____

_____

_____

**5.** How are Uranus and Neptune alike and different? _____

_____

_____

_____

**6.** Which planets are rocky? Which are called the gas giants? _____

_____

_____

Harcourt

Name _____

Date _____

# Telescopes

## Materials

**1 thin (eyepiece) lens**

**1 thick (objective) lens**

**small piece of modeling clay**

**small-diameter cardboard tube**

**large-diameter cardboard tube**

## CAUTION | Activity Procedure

**1** Press small pieces of clay to the outside of the thin lens. Then put the lens in one end of the small tube. Use enough clay to hold the lens in place, keeping the lens as straight as possible. Be careful not to smear the middle of the lens with clay.

**2** Repeat Step 1 using the thick lens and large tube.

**3** Slide the open end of the small tube into the larger tube. You have just made a telescope.

**4** Hold your telescope up, and look through one lens. Then turn the telescope around, and look through the other lens. **CAUTION** **Never look directly at the sun.** Slide the small tube in and out of the large tube until what you see is in focus, or not blurry. How do objects appear through each lens? **Record** your **observations**.

My observations: _____

_____

_____

Harcourt

Investigate Log

## Draw Conclusions

1. What did you **observe** as you looked through each lens? _____

_____

_____

_____

2. Using your observations, **infer** which lens you should look through to **observe** the stars. Explain your answer. _____

_____

_____

_____

3. **Scientists at Work** Astronomers (uh•STRAWN•uh•merz) are scientists who study objects in space. Some astronomers use large telescopes with many parts to **observe** objects in space. How would your telescope make observing objects in the night sky easier? _____

_____

_____

_____

**Investigate Further** Use your telescope to observe the moon at night. Make a list of the details you can see using your telescope that you can't see using only your eyes. _____

_____

_____

_____

_____

Harcourt

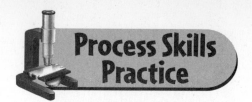

# Observe

Telescopes can help you observe details of objects in the solar system.

## Think About Observing

Look at the drawings of Jupiter. The larger one was based on a photograph taken through a telescope.

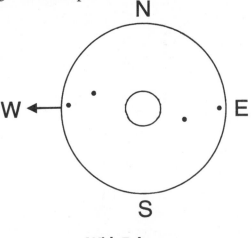

**With Telescope**

**Without Telescope**

1. What does Jupiter look like when viewed with the eyes alone?

   _____

2. What does Jupiter look like when viewed through a telescope?

   _____

   _____

3. What features can you see with the telescope that you cannot see without the

   telescope? List at least two features. _____

   _____

4. The small dots spreading out in a line near Jupiter are the planet's four largest moons. Italian scientist Galileo Galilei was the first person to observe these moons through a telescope. He watched them change position over the course of a few days and inferred that the moons revolved around Jupiter. What do you think Galileo observed that caused him to make this inference?

   _____

   _____

**Use with page D69.**

Harcourt

Concept Review

# How Do People Study the Solar System?

## Lesson Concept

People use different kinds of telescopes, as well as crewed missions and space probes, to study the solar system.

## Vocabulary

**telescope** (D70)                    **space probe** (D74)

**Answer the questions below about how people study the solar system.**

**1.** How are these two telescopes different? _____

_____

_____

**2.** What kinds of problems occur with optical telescopes? List three ways scientists

have worked around these problems. _____

_____

_____

_____

_____

**3.** What is the difference between a crewed mission and a space probe?

_____

_____

Harcourt

# Constellations

## Materials

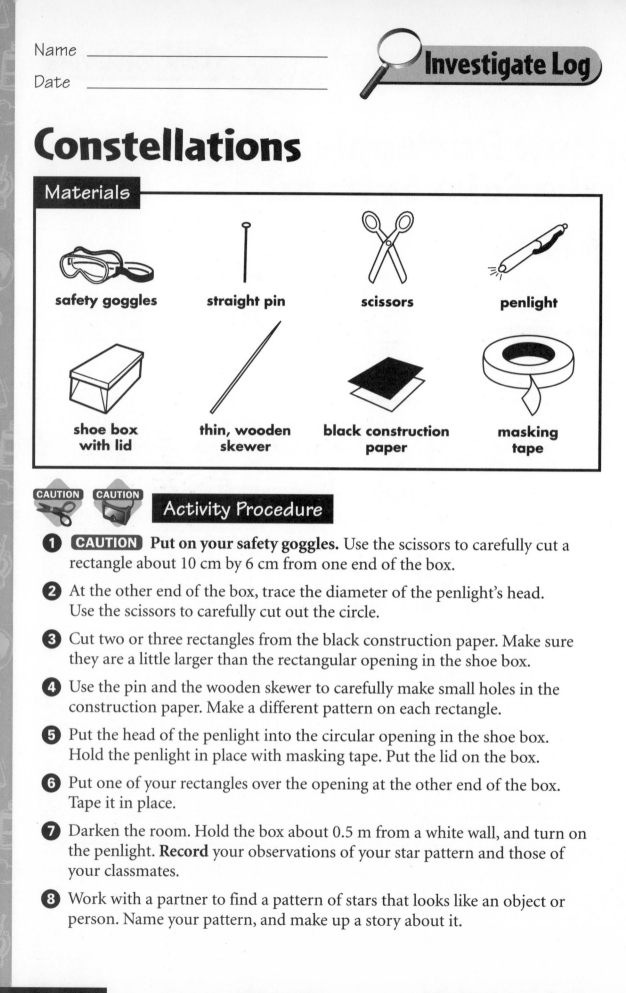

safety goggles

straight pin

scissors

penlight

shoe box with lid

thin, wooden skewer

black construction paper

masking tape

**CAUTION** **CAUTION** **Activity Procedure**

❶ **CAUTION** **Put on your safety goggles.** Use the scissors to carefully cut a rectangle about 10 cm by 6 cm from one end of the box.

❷ At the other end of the box, trace the diameter of the penlight's head. Use the scissors to carefully cut out the circle.

❸ Cut two or three rectangles from the black construction paper. Make sure they are a little larger than the rectangular opening in the shoe box.

❹ Use the pin and the wooden skewer to carefully make small holes in the construction paper. Make a different pattern on each rectangle.

❺ Put the head of the penlight into the circular opening in the shoe box. Hold the penlight in place with masking tape. Put the lid on the box.

❻ Put one of your rectangles over the opening at the other end of the box. Tape it in place.

❼ Darken the room. Hold the box about 0.5 m from a white wall, and turn on the penlight. **Record** your observations of your star pattern and those of your classmates.

❽ Work with a partner to find a pattern of stars that looks like an object or person. Name your pattern, and make up a story about it.

Harcourt

Name _____

## Draw Conclusions

**1.** What did the star patterns look like? _____

_____

_____

_____

**2.** Could you find a group of "stars" that looked like the shape of an object or person? These patterns found among the stars are called constellations.

Describe your constellation. _____

_____

_____

_____

_____

**3. Scientists at Work** Not all stars are the same distance from Earth. Also, not all stars shine with the same brightness. Think about your **model**. What do you

think the larger holes stand for? _____

_____

What do the smaller holes stand for? _____

_____

_____

**Investigate Further** Again, project your star pattern on the wall, this time with the lights on. How does what you see in the light compare with what you saw in

the dark? _____

_____

**Infer** why you can't see most stars during the day. _____

_____

_____

Harcourt

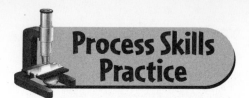

# Process Skills Practice

# Make a Model

Making models of star patterns, or constellations, can help you find the constellations in the night sky.

### Think About Making a Model

Kai-Ming read about the constellation called Orion. He made a map of the constellation to help him find the star pattern in the night sky. Answer the following questions regarding Kai-Ming's map.

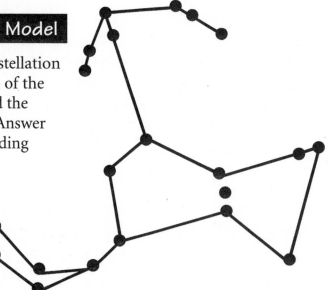

1. The brightest star in the constellation Orion is Betelgeuse. Identifying Betelgeuse could help Kai-Ming locate Orion in the sky. How could Kai-Ming show on his map that Betelguese is the brightest star? Give two ways.

   _____

   _____

   _____

2. Betelgeuse is a red star. Rigel, the second brightest star in Orion, is a blue star. How could Kai-Ming show this on his map? How could this help him as he

   tries to find the constellation Orion? _____

   _____

   _____

3. The three stars close together in the middle of the constellation are bright and easy to spot. They are called Orion's belt. How could Kai-Ming add this information to his map as an aid for finding the constellation? Give two ways.

   _____

   _____

   _____

Harcourt

Name _____

Date _____

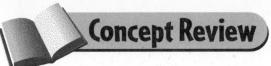
**Concept Review**

# What Are Constellations?

Constellations are patterns of stars in the sky.

**Vocabulary**

**constellation** (D78)

**Write the letter of the best response on the line that best answers the question or completes the sentence.**

1. Why do many stars appear to rise in the east and set in the west? _____
   **A** because Earth rotates on its axis
   **B** because Earth revolves around the sun
   **C** because the stars are part of seasonal constellations

2. Why do different stars appear in the sky at different times of the year? _____
   **A** because Earth rotates on its axis
   **B** because Earth revolves around the sun
   **C** because the stars are moving in their galaxies

3. How is the North Star different from most other stars? _____
   **A** It appears to move across the sky from north to south.
   **B** It appears to move across the sky from south to north.
   **C** It does not appear to move across the sky.

4. What are the circumpolar stars? _____
   **A** stars that appear to travel around the North Star
   **B** stars that appear to travel around the South Star
   **C** stars that appear to rise in the east and set in the west

5. In the Northern Hemisphere, people use the North Star to tell which direction is north. What do they use in the Southern Hemisphere? _____
   **A** the South Star
   **B** the Southern Cross
   **C** the Big Dipper

Harcourt

# Recognize Vocabulary

Pretend that your cousins won an exciting vacation through our solar system and beyond. They sent you a letter describing what they saw. For every set of italicized words, write the correct vocabulary term that matches it.

| | | | |
|---|---|---|---|
| solar system | star | planet | asteroid |
| comet | orbit | axis | inner planet |
| outer planet | gas giant | telescope | space probe |
| constellation | | | |

Our tour started close to the sun. The tour guide told us that the sun was

really a _____, *a burning sphere of gases.* After we flew

around the sun, we visited the _____, *the four planets closest to the sun.* We passed Mercury, which we watched speeding in its *path*

*around the sun,* or its _____. Did you know that Mercury goes around once every 88 days? We flew on past Venus. We got a good view of Earth

and we stopped to look through a _____, *a device people use to make distant objects appear closer.* It was traveling around Earth, taking pictures of stars. After we went past Mars, we flew by some *small rocky objects,*

_____. Our tour guide told us we would soon be visiting the

_____, *the five planets farthest from the sun.* She said that four of

these planets are _____, *large spheres made mostly of gases.* The first one we saw, Jupiter, was spinning so fast, it looked like a top turning on

*the line running through its center,* its _____. We went on past Saturn and Uranus. We saw an *object carrying cameras and other instruments,*

called a(n) _____, heading toward Neptune. We also swung by

a(n) _____, *a small mass of dust and ice.* Once we pass Pluto, we

will head toward the _____, or *star pattern* of Leo. We hope to

see another _____, *a group of objects in space that move around*

*a central star.* We're searching for different _____, *large objects that move around stars.*

Harcourt

# Chapter 1 • Graphic Organizer for Chapter Concepts

## Physical Properties of Matter

### LESSON 1
### STATES OF MATTER

Three States and How They Are Different

1. has a definite shape

2. takes up a definite amount of space

3. particles move back and forth around a point

___

1. takes the shape of its container

2. takes up a definite amount of space

3. particles slip and slide past each other

___

1. no definite shape or volume

2. particles move freely and rapidly in all directions

### LESSON 2
### MEASURING AND COMPARING MATTER

Properties of Matter That Can Be Measured

1. _____

2. _____

3. _____

How Matter Is Measured

1. _____

2. _____

3. _____

### LESSON 3
### USEFUL PROPERTIES OF MATTER

Useful Properties

1. _____

2. _____

# Physical Properties of Matter

## Materials

| | | |
|---|---|---|
| plastic bag | plastic drinking straw | book |

## Activity Procedure

**1** Wrap the opening of the plastic bag tightly around the straw. Use your fingers to hold the bag in place.

**2** Blow into the straw. **Observe** what happens to the bag.

**My observations:** _____

_____

**3** Empty the bag. Now place a book on the bag. Again wrap the opening of the bag tightly around the straw and use your fingers to hold the bag in place.

**4** **Predict** what will happen when you blow into the straw. Blow into it and **observe** what happens to the book.

**My prediction:** _____

_____

**My observations:** _____

_____

Harcourt

## Draw Conclusions

1. What happened to the bag when you blew air into it? _____

_____

What happened to the book? _____

_____

2. What property of air caused the effects you observed in Steps 2 and 4?

_____

_____

3. **Scientists at Work** Scientists **draw conclusions** after they think carefully about observations and other data they have collected. What data supports your answer to Question 2 above? _____

_____

_____

**Investigate Further** In a sink, place a filled 1-L bottle on an empty plastic bag. Use a tube connected to a faucet to slowly fill the bag with water. What happens to the bottle when the bag fills with water? _____

_____

_____

What property of water do you **observe**? _____

_____

_____

Harcourt

Name _____

Date _____

# Draw Conclusions

You draw conclusions after you collect and analyze data. Your data should give strong support for the conclusions you draw.

## Think About Drawing Conclusions

Gunter measured a cup of water. He poured the water into a small mixing bowl. Then he poured it into a tall vase. Then he poured it into a pie pan. He was careful not to spill any of the water as he poured it from one container to another. The pictures show what the water looked like in each of these containers.

Next, Gunter poured the water from the pie pan back into the measuring cup. He noted the level of the water was one cup. He put a half-cup measuring cup in the pie pan and poured the water into the measuring cup. The water filled the half-cup measuring cup and spilled over into the pie pan.

1. Based on this experiment, what could Gunter conclude about the shape a liquid will take? Give evidence to support this conclusion.

_____

_____

_____

_____

2. The volume of a substance is the amount of space that the substance takes up. What can Gunter conclude about the volume of a liquid, based on this

experiment? Give evidence to support this conclusion. _____

_____

_____

_____

_____

_____

_____

Harcourt

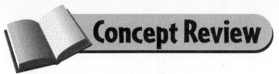

# What Are Three States of Matter?

## Lesson Concept

Solids, liquids, and gases are three states of matter.

## Vocabulary

**matter** (E6)    **mass** (E6)    **solid** (E6)    **liquid** (E7)    **gas** (E8)

What is matter? _____

**Fill in the chart below.**

| Characteristic/ Description | Solid | Liquid | Gas |
|---|---|---|---|
| Has definite shape | | | |
| Takes up a definite amount of space | | | |
| How particles are arranged | | | |
| How particles move | | | |
| Cools off to become | | | |
| Heats up to become | | | |
| Examples | | | |

Harcourt

# Density

## Materials

raisins  pan balance  3 identical plastic cups  breakfast cereal

## Activity Procedure

1. Fill one cup with raisins. Make sure the raisins fill the cup all the way to the top.

2. Fill another cup with cereal. Make sure the cereal fills the cup all the way to the top.

3. **Observe** the amount of space taken up by the raisins and the cereal.

   **My observations:** _____

   _____

4. Adjust the balance so the pans are level. Place one cup on each pan. **Observe** what happens.

   **My observations:** _____

   _____

5. Fill the third cup with a mixture of raisins and cereal. **Predict** how the mass of the cup of raisins and cereal will compare with the masses of the cup of raisins and the cup of cereal. Use the balance to check your predictions.

   **My prediction:** _____

   _____

   _____

Harcourt

## Draw Conclusions

1. **Compare** the amount of space taken up by the raisins with the space taken up by the cereal. _____

   _____

2. Which has more mass, the cup of raisins or the cup of cereal? Explain your answer. _____

   _____

   _____

3. Which cup has more matter packed into it? Explain your answer.

   _____

   _____

   _____

   _____

4. **Scientists at Work** It is important to know the starting place when you measure. What would happen if you **measured** without making the balance pans equal? Explain your answer. _____

   _____

   _____

   _____

**Investigate Further** Write step-by-step directions to **compare** the masses of any two materials and the space they take up. Exchange sets of directions with a classmate. Test the directions and suggest revisions. _____

_____

_____

_____

_____

_____

_____

Harcourt

Name _____

Date _____

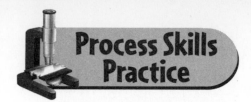

# Measure

Measuring involves making observations using numbers. When you use tools, such as balances, to measure, you need to make sure the tools work properly.

### Think About Measuring

**1.** Do the cup and the block have the same mass? Explain how you decided.

_____

_____

**2.** Do the dark ball and the light ball have the same mass? Explain how you

decided. _____

_____

Angela wanted to measure the mass and the space taken up by two different liquids. She took two measuring cups and poured a half cup of one liquid in one cup and a half cup of the other liquid in the second cup. She leveled the balance pans and placed one cup on one balance pan and the second cup on the second balance pan.

**3.** Do the liquids take up the same amount of space? _____

**4.** Do the liquids have the same amount of mass? _____

**Use with page E11.**

Harcourt

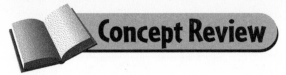

# How Can Matter Be Measured and Compared?

## Lesson Concept

An object's mass, volume, and density tell you how much matter it has.

## Vocabulary

**volume** (E13)          **density** (E14)

Use the illustrations below to help you answer the questions.

**A. graduate**

**B. calculator**

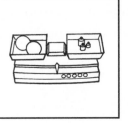

**C. balance**

**D. ruler**

**1.** Which tool would you use to measure mass? Explain how to use the tool.

_____

_____

_____

**2.** Which tool would you use to measure a liquid's volume? Explain how to use the tool. _____

_____

**3.** Which tool would you use to measure the volume of a solid with a regular shape, such as a box? Explain how to use the tool. _____

_____

**4.** Once you know an object's mass and volume, which tool would you use to find its density? Explain how to use the tool. _____

_____

Harcourt

# Floating and Sinking

## Materials

plastic shoe box     sheet of aluminum foil     water     modeling clay

## Activity Procedure

**1** Fill the plastic shoe box halfway with water.

**2** Take a small sheet of aluminum foil about 10 cm long and 10 cm wide. Squeeze it tightly into a ball. Before placing the ball in the shoe box, **predict** whether it will sink or float. Test your prediction, and **record** your **observations**.

**My prediction:** _____

**My observations:** _____

**3** Take a thin piece of modeling clay about 10 cm long and 10 cm wide. Squeeze it tightly into a ball. Place the ball in the shoe box. **Observe** whether it sinks or floats.

**My observations:** _____

**4** Uncurl the foil. Use it to make a boat. Before placing the boat on the water, **predict** whether it will sink or float. Test your prediction, and **record** your **observations**.

**My prediction:** _____

**My observations:** _____

**5** Make a boat out of the modeling clay. Before placing the boat on the water, **predict** whether it will sink or float. Test your prediction, and **record** your **observations**.

**My prediction:** _____

**My observations:** _____

Harcourt

Name _____

## Draw Conclusions

**1.** Which objects floated? _____

_____

_____

_____

Which objects sank? _____

**2.** Which do you think has the greater density, the ball of aluminum foil or the
ball of modeling clay? Explain. _____

_____

_____

_____

_____

**3. Scientists at Work** Scientists often look at two situations in which everything
is the same except for one property. What property was the same in Step 3 as
in Step 5? _____

_____

What property was different in Step 3 and Step 5? _____

_____

_____

What can you **infer** about how that difference changed the results?

_____

_____

_____

**Investigate Further** Poke a hole of the same size in the bottom of each boat. Put
both boats in the water. What happens? _____

_____

_____

_____

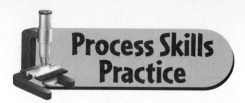

# Infer

When you infer, you sometimes use observations or data from an experiment as a basis for your inferences.

## Think About Inferring

Anthony compared how much water different objects displaced, the objects' masses, the masses of the water displaced, and whether the objects floated or sank. The table below shows the data he collected. For the experiment, Anthony assumed that the water had a density of 1 g/cm³.

| Object | Mass of Object | Volume of Water Displaced | Mass of Water Displaced | Whether Object Floated or Sank |
|---|---|---|---|---|
| Barrette (plastic) | 4 g | 4 cm³ | 4 g | Floated |
| Marble | 28 g | 10 cm³ | 10 g | Sank |
| Orange peel | 9 g | 9 cm³ | 9 g | Floated |

1. Anthony measured the mass of each object and the volume of water that each object displaced. How do you think Anthony figured out the mass of the water

   displaced? _____

   _____

2. Based on the data in the table, would you infer that a metal clip that has a mass of 25 g and displaces 6 cm³ of water would float or sink? Explain your answer.

   _____

   _____

   _____

3. Would you infer that 10 g of cereal in a small plastic bag that displaces 10 cm³ of water would float or sink? Explain your answer based on the data in the

   table. _____

   _____

   _____

Harcourt

Name _____

Date _____

**Concept Review**

# What Are Some Useful Properties of Matter?

When solids interact with liquids, the solids may or may not dissolve; solids, liquids, and gases can float or sink in other liquids or gases.

**Vocabulary**

**solution** (E18)    **dissolve** (E19)    **solubility** (E19)    **buoyancy** (E20)

**Answer the questions below.**

1. Circle from the list below the materials that dissolve in water.
   sand        sugar        salt        food coloring        plastic

2. What happens when a solid dissolves in a liquid? _____
   _____

3. What is solubility? _____
   _____

4. What is buoyancy? _____

5. Circle the things that sink in water.
   pine wood        lead weight        sand        oil        maple syrup        air

6. Why do the circled objects in Question 5 sink in water? _____
   _____

7. Why do the uncircled objects in Question 5 float? _____
   _____

8. How can you make something that sinks float? _____
   _____

9. How can you make something that floats sink? _____

Harcourt

Name _____

Date _____

# Recognize Vocabulary

Use the clues to fill in the word puzzle with the terms in the box.

| | | |
|---|---|---|
| matter | mass | solid |
| liquid | gas | volume |
| density | solution | dissolve |
| solubility | buoyancy | |

**Across**

2. different particles of matter mixed evenly

3. salt will ____ in water to form a solution

5. matter that takes the shape of its container and takes up a definite amount of space

8. the ability of matter to float in a liquid or gas

9. matter that has a definite shape and takes up a definite amount of space

10. has mass and takes up space

**Down**

1. matter that has no definite shape and takes up no definite amount of space

2. the amount of a material that will dissolve in another material

4. the amount of space that matter takes up

6. the amount of matter compared to the space it takes up

7. the amount of matter something contains

Harcourt

# Chapter 2 • Graphic Organizer for Chapter Concepts

## Heat—Energy on the Move

### LESSON 1
### UNDERSTANDING
### THERMAL ENERGY

What It Is _____

How It's Measured _____

_____

What Happens When Thermal
Energy Is Added To Matter

_____

What Happens When Thermal
Energy Is Taken Away

_____

### LESSON 2
### TRANSFERRING
### THERMAL ENERGY

The process of transferring thermal

energy is _____

Three Ways Thermal Energy Can Be
Transferred

1. _____

_____

_____

2. _____

_____

3. _____

### LESSON 3
### PRODUCING AND
### USING THERMAL ENERGY

How Thermal Energy Is Produced

1. _____

2. _____

How Thermal Energy Is Used

1. _____

2. _____

3. _____

# Changes in a Heated Ballon

## Materials

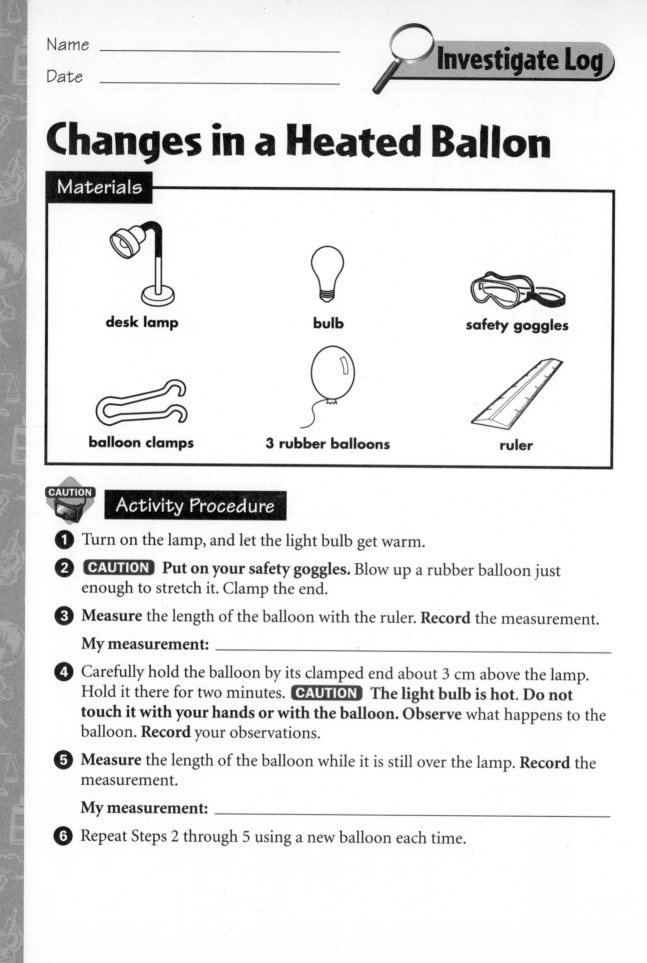

desk lamp

bulb

safety goggles

balloon clamps

3 rubber balloons

ruler

## ⚠️CAUTION Activity Procedure

**1** Turn on the lamp, and let the light bulb get warm.

**2** **CAUTION** **Put on your safety goggles.** Blow up a rubber balloon just enough to stretch it. Clamp the end.

**3** **Measure** the length of the balloon with the ruler. **Record** the measurement.

**My measurement:** _____

**4** Carefully hold the balloon by its clamped end about 3 cm above the lamp. Hold it there for two minutes. **CAUTION** **The light bulb is hot. Do not touch it with your hands or with the balloon. Observe** what happens to the balloon. **Record** your observations.

**5** **Measure** the length of the balloon while it is still over the lamp. **Record** the measurement.

**My measurement:** _____

**6** Repeat Steps 2 through 5 using a new balloon each time.

Harcourt

Name _____

## Draw Conclusions

1. What did you **observe** as you warmed the balloons? _____

_____

2. **Compare** the lengths of the heated balloons with the lengths of the unheated

balloons. _____

_____

3. What can you **infer** happened to the air inside the balloons as you heated it?

_____

_____

4. **Scientists at Work** Scientists often **measure** several times to make sure the
   measurements are accurate. In this investigation you measured the lengths of
   three different balloons. Were the measurements all the same? Explain.

_____

_____

_____

_____

_____

**Investigate Further** Fill a balloon with water that is at room temperature. Put the
balloon on a desk and **measure** its length. Heat the balloon by putting it in a bowl
of hot tap water for 15 minutes. Take the balloon out of the bowl and measure its
length. **Compare** these lengths with the lengths you measured with the air-filled

balloons in the investigation. _____

_____

Harcourt

Name _____

Date _____

# Measure

Making careful measurements can help you find useful patterns in data.

## Think About Measuring

The staff at a construction supply store noticed changes in some of the materials at different seasons. They decided to take careful measurements and record what they learned. Their data is presented in the table below.

| Material | Length (in meters) at ⁻15°C | Length (in meters) at 10°C | Length (in meters) at 35°C |
|---|---|---|---|
| Brass piping | 19.991 | 20.000 | 20.010 |
| Copper wire | 99.958 | 100.000 | 100.040 |
| Plate glass | 11.997 | 12.000 | 12.003 |
| Rubber matting | 49.990 | 50.000 | 50.100 |
| Steel beam | 9.9973 | 10.000 | 10.003 |

1. What trends do these measurements of different materials show?

_____

_____

2. Do you think it would be easy to measure changes to kilometer-long lengths of copper cable during hot summer weather? Explain. _____

_____

_____

_____

3. Based on this data, what would you expect to happen to the meter-square rubber mats under playground equipment during cold winter weather? Do you think it would be easy to measure any changes? Explain. _____

_____

_____

Harcourt

# How Does Heat Affect Matter?

**Lesson Concept**

Thermal energy is the energy of motion of particles in matter. Heat is the process of transferring thermal energy.

**Vocabulary**

| | | |
|---|---|---|
| **energy** (E34) | **thermal energy** (E34) | **temperature** (E35) |

**Fill in the blanks.**

**1.** To move, an object requires _____.

**2.** Particles in matter are always moving. These particles have

_____.

**3.** The particles in a hot object move _____ than those in a colder object.

**4.** A measure of the average thermal energy of the particles moving in matter is

called _____.

**5.** The instrument used to measure average thermal energy is a

_____.

**6.** When you _____ thermal energy to an object, the object's particles move faster.

**7.** If you add enough thermal energy, a material may change its

_____.

**8.** Two objects may have the same temperature, but they will not have the same amounts of thermal energy unless they also have the same amount of

_____.

**9.** It would take more thermal energy to heat up a _____

pan of water than a _____ pan of water.

Harcourt

# Hot Air

## Materials

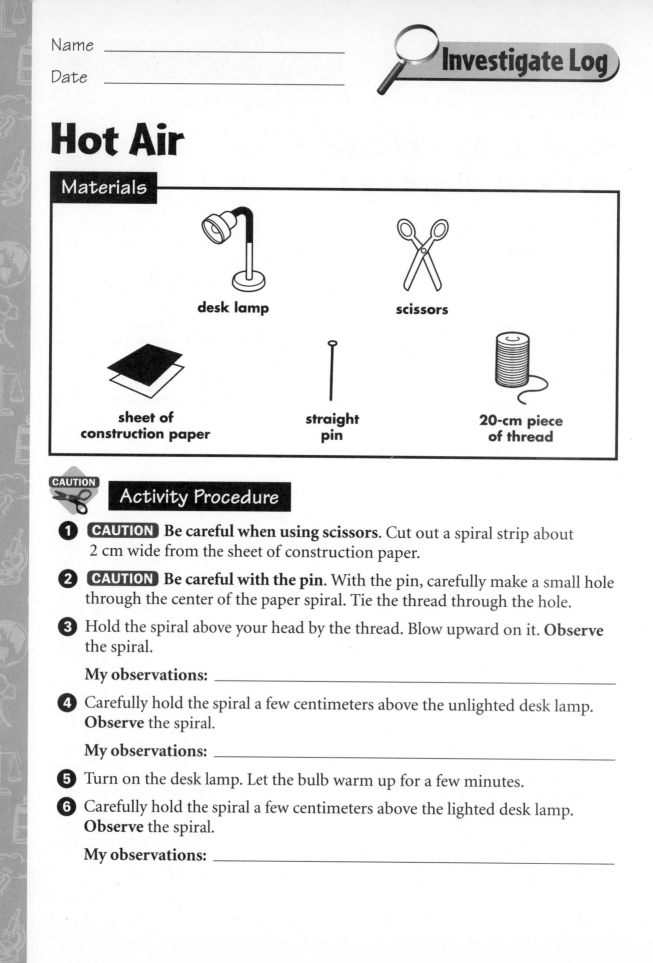

desk lamp

scissors

sheet of
construction paper

straight
pin

20-cm piece
of thread

### Activity Procedure

**CAUTION**

1. **CAUTION** **Be careful when using scissors.** Cut out a spiral strip about 2 cm wide from the sheet of construction paper.

2. **CAUTION** **Be careful with the pin.** With the pin, carefully make a small hole through the center of the paper spiral. Tie the thread through the hole.

3. Hold the spiral above your head by the thread. Blow upward on it. **Observe** the spiral.

   **My observations:** _____

4. Carefully hold the spiral a few centimeters above the unlighted desk lamp. **Observe** the spiral.

   **My observations:** _____

5. Turn on the desk lamp. Let the bulb warm up for a few minutes.

6. Carefully hold the spiral a few centimeters above the lighted desk lamp. **Observe** the spiral.

   **My observations:** _____

Harcourt

## Draw Conclusions

**1.** What did you **observe** in Steps 3, 4, and 6? _____

_____

_____

_____

_____

**2.** What caused the result you **observed** in Step 3? _____

_____

_____

_____

_____

**3.** What was different about Steps 4 and 6? _____

_____

_____

_____

_____

**4.** **Scientists at Work** Scientists often **infer** from **observations** a cause that they can't see directly. What do you think caused the result you observed in Step 6?

_____

_____

_____

_____

**Investigate Further** Hold the spiral a few centimeters away from the side of the lighted desk lamp. **Observe** the spiral. What can you **infer** from your observation?

_____

_____

_____

_____

Harcourt

Name _____

Date _____

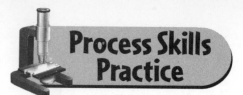

# Observe and Infer

Observing involves using your senses to collect information; inferring involves using those observations to come up with ideas about what caused the things you observed.

## Think About Observing and Inferring

Beth had one helium balloon left from her party. A few days after the party, Beth noticed that the balloon was floating around in the middle of the room. Her father explained that some of the helium in the balloon had been replaced with air. This made the balloon about the same density as air, so it floated. But he didn't explain the strange pattern it followed. The balloon would rise near the radiator and float up toward the ceiling. From there, it would travel near the ceiling to the opposite wall of the room near the window. Then the balloon would sink to the floor. It would travel along the floor until it came close to the radiator, again. There it would rise again and retrace its circular journey.

1. Trace the path that Beth observed the balloon following.

2. What would you infer caused the balloon to move? On what do you base this

   inference? _____

   _____

   _____

3. Beth observed that the air near the radiator felt warmer than the air near the window. Use this observation and other experiences you have had to make an inference about how such temperature differences could cause Beth's balloon

   to move. _____

   _____

   _____

   _____

   _____

   _____

Name _____

Date _____

# How Can Thermal Energy Be Transferred?

## Lesson Concept

Thermal energy can be transferred in three ways—convection, conduction, and radiation.

## Vocabulary

| | | |
|---|---|---|
| **heat** (E40) | **conduction** (E41) | **convection** (E42) |
| **radiation** (E44) | **infrared radiation** (E44) | |

**Answer the questions below about thermal energy.**

1. Show how thermal energy can travel through a pot on a stove to the water inside. Write captions for your pictures.

_____   _____   _____
_____   _____   _____
_____   _____   _____
_____   _____   _____
_____   _____   _____

2. Show how thermal energy can travel from the sun through outer space to Earth. Write captions for your pictures.

_____   _____   _____
_____   _____   _____
_____   _____   _____

Harcourt

Name _____

Date _____

# Temperatures in a Solar Cooker

## Materials

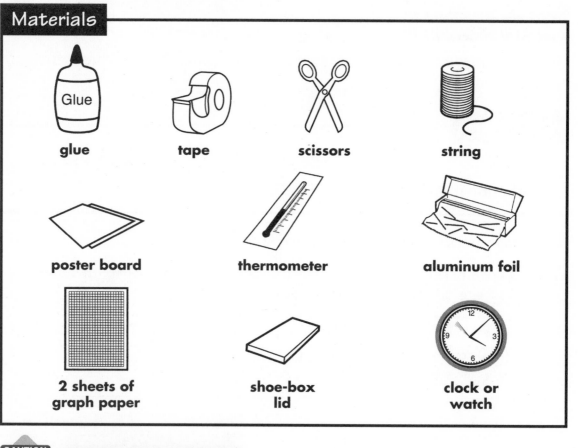

glue    tape    scissors    string

poster board    thermometer    aluminum foil

2 sheets of graph paper    shoe-box lid    clock or watch

CAUTION

## Activity Procedure

1. Label the two sheets of graph paper like the one shown on page E47.

2. Tape a piece of foil into the shoe-box lid. Place the thermometer in the lid.

3. Place the lid in sunlight. **Record** the temperature immediately. Then record the temperature each minute for 10 minutes.

4. In the shade, remove the thermometer from the shoe-box lid.

5. Cut a rectangle of poster board 10 cm by 30 cm. Glue foil to one side. Let the glue dry for 10 minutes.

6. **CAUTION** **Be careful when using scissors**. Carefully use scissors to punch a hole about 2 cm from each end of the rectangle. Make a curved reflector by drawing the poster board ends toward each other with string until they are about 20 cm apart. Tie the string.

Harcourt

**7** Put the curved reflector in the shoe-box lid. Put the thermometer in the center of the curve. Repeat Step 3.

**8** Make a line graph of the measurements in Step 3. Make another line graph of the measurements in Step 7.

## Draw Conclusions

1. Describe the temperature changes shown on each graph. _____

_____

2. **Compare** the temperature changes shown on the two graphs. _____

_____

3. **Infer** what may have caused the differences in the temperatures on the two

graphs. _____

_____

4. **Scientists at Work** How does **displaying the data** in a graph help you

**interpret** what happened to the temperature in Steps 3 and 7? _____

_____

Harcourt

Name _____

Date _____

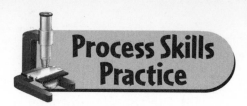

# Interpret Data

Interpreting data involves looking at data closely and finding
relationships or patterns in the data.

## Think About Interpreting Data

Gertrude made a solar oven. She used it to cook several different
foods. She kept track of the cooking times with the solar oven and
compared them with the cooking times for the same foods in a
conventional oven. The graph below shows her results.

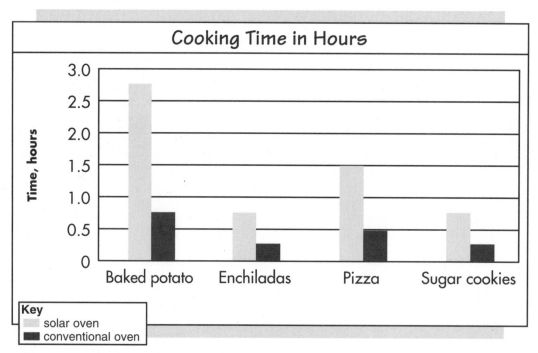

**Cooking Time in Hours**

1. How long did it take Gertrude's enchiladas to cook in her solar oven? How long
   would they take to cook in a conventional oven? _____

   _____

2. What relationship do you see between the cooking times for a solar oven and
   the cooking times for a conventional oven? _____

   _____

3. How does displaying the data in a bar graph help you interpret the data about
   the cooking times? _____

   _____

Harcourt   **Use with page E47.**

# How Is Thermal Energy Produced and Used?

## Lesson Concept

Thermal energy is useful in many ways. It is considered waste heat if it is not used.

## Vocabulary

| | |
|---|---|
| **fuel** (E48) | **solar energy** (E49) |

**Fill in the chart about uses of different types of thermal energy.**

| Method of Producing Energy | Examples of Use of This Energy | Advantages of Producing Energy This Way | Disadvantages of Producing Energy This Way |
|---|---|---|---|
| Burning wood | | | |
| Burning coal | | | |
| Burning fuel or gasoline | | | |
| Focusing solar energy | | | |

Harcourt

# Recognize Vocabulary

**Write the letter of the choice that best completes the sentence.**

1. The ability to cause change in objects or materials is called _____.

   **A** friction       **B** heat       **C** energy

2. Any material that can burn is _____.

   **A** carbon       **B** oxygen       **C** a fuel

3. Thermal energy is _____.

   **A** the energy of the motion of particles in matter

   **B** the motion of particles from one part of matter to another

   **C** the boiling of water

4. The transfer of thermal energy is _____.

   **A** conduction       **B** heat       **C** convection

5. We call the transfer of thermal energy from particles bumping into each other _____.

   **A** conduction       **B** convection       **C** radiation

6. We call the transfer of thermal energy as particles in gases or liquids move from one place to another _____.

   **A** conduction       **B** convection       **C** radiation

7. The transfer of energy through empty space happens by _____.

   **A** conduction       **B** convection       **C** radiation

8. Bundles of energy that transfer heat through empty space as well as through matter are called _____.

   **A** solar energy       **B** infrared radiation       **C** light

9. The measure of the average energy of motion in matter is known as _____.

   **A** solar energy       **B** heat       **C** temperature

10. The energy given off by the sun alone is called _____.

    **A** solar energy       **B** infrared radiation       **C** thermal energy

Harcourt

# Chapter 3 • Graphic Organizer for Chapter Concepts

## Sound

### LESSON 1
### UNDERSTANDING SOUND

Causes of Sound _____
_____

Sound Waves Move
1. _____
2. _____

Sound Waves Travel Through
1. _____
2. _____
3. _____

We Hear Sounds With Our _____

The Three Parts of These Organs
1. _____
2. _____
3. _____

### LESSON 2
### SOUNDS VARY

Loudness Depends On
1. _____
2. _____

Pitch Depends On
1. _____

Pitch Can Be Changed By Changing
1. _____
2. _____

### LESSON 3
### HOW SOUND TRAVELS

The Speed of Sound In Air Is _____

Sound Waves Can
1. _____
2. _____
3. _____

# Sound from a Ruler

## Materials

plastic ruler

## Activity Procedure

**1** Place the ruler on a tabletop. Let 15 to 20 cm stick out over the edge of the table.

**2** Hold the ruler tightly against the tabletop with one hand. Use the thumb of your other hand to flick, or strum, the free end of the ruler.

**3** **Observe** the ruler with your eyes. **Record** your observations.

**My observations:** _____

_____

**4** Repeat Step 2. **Observe** the ruler with your ears. **Record** your observations.

**My observations:** _____

_____

**5** Flick the ruler harder. **Observe** the results. **Record** your observations.

**My observations:** _____

_____

**6** Change the length of the ruler sticking over the edge of the table, and repeat Steps 2 through 5. **Observe** the results. **Record** your observations.

**My observations:** _____

_____

Harcourt

Name _____

## Draw Conclusions

1. What did you **observe** in Step 3? _____

2. What did you **observe** in Step 4? _____

3. **Make a hypothesis** to explain what you **observed** in Steps 3 and 4. How could

   you test your explanation? _____

   _____

4. **Scientists at Work**  When scientists want to learn more about an experiment,
   they change one part of it and **observe** the effect. What did you change in

   Step 6? _____

   What effect did you observe? _____

**Investigate Further**  Place one ear on the tabletop. Cover the other ear with your
hand. Have a partner repeat Steps 1 and 2. What do you **observe**?

_____

_____

Harcourt

Name _____

Date _____

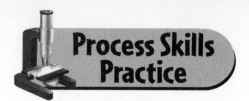

# Observe

Observing involves using your senses, including hearing and touch, to notice things that occur.

## Think About Observing

Miguel decided he wanted to learn how a guitar makes sound. Miguel held a guitar in his lap and plucked the bottom string. He felt the string vibrate and heard it make a sound. Then he plucked the other strings. Each string made a different sound. He noticed each string had a different thickness. The thin strings made high-pitched sounds, and the thick strings made low-pitched sounds.

1. Write in the appropriate boxes the observations Miguel made using his senses of sight, hearing, and touch.

| Sight | Hearing | Touch |
|-------|---------|-------|
|       |         |       |
|       |         |       |
|       |         |       |
|       |         |       |

2. Based on his observations, what hypothesis might Miguel make about how the guitar makes sound? _____

_____

3. What are two ways Miguel might account for the differences he noticed among the sounds the strings made? _____

_____

Harcourt

# What Is Sound?

## Lesson Concept

Sound is made by vibrating objects.

## Vocabulary

**sound** (E62)          **compression** (E63)          **sound wave** (E63)

**Answer the questions about sound below.**

**1.** Give a definition of sound. _____

**2.** What are three ways you can detect sound? _____

_____

**Label the diagram, using the words below.**

| hammer, anvil, stirrup | middle ear | brain | outer ear |
| area of low pressure | compression | inner ear | eardrum |
| cochlea | sound wave | | |

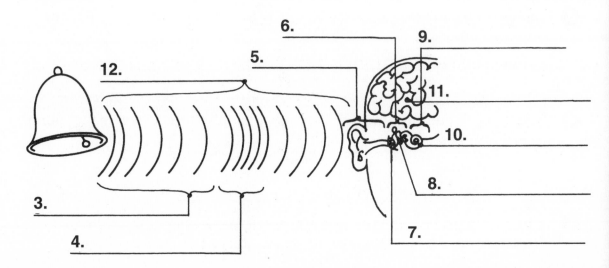

# Making Different Sounds

## Materials

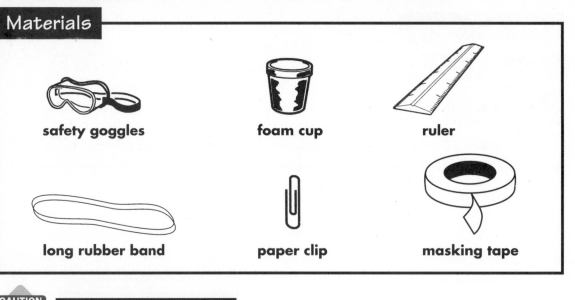

safety goggles

foam cup

ruler

long rubber band

paper clip

masking tape

### Activity Procedure

**CAUTION**

1. **CAUTION** **Put on the safety goggles.** With a pencil, punch a small hole in the bottom of the cup. Thread the rubber band through the paper clip. Put the paper clip inside the cup, and pull the rubber band through the hole.

2. Turn the cup upside down on a table. Stand the ruler on the table next to it, with the 1-cm mark at the top. Tape one side of the cup to the ruler. Pull the rubber band over the top of the ruler, and tape it to the back.

3. Pull the rubber band to one side, and let it go. **Observe** the sound. **Record** your observations.

   **My observations:** _____

   _____

4. Repeat Step 3, but this time pull the rubber band farther. **Observe** the sound. **Record** your observations.

   **My observations:** _____

   _____

5. With one finger, hold the rubber band down to the ruler at the 4-cm mark. Pluck the rubber band. **Observe** the sound. **Record** your observations.

   **My observations:** _____

   _____

Harcourt

**6** Repeat Step 5, but this time hold the
rubber band down at the 6-cm mark. Then do this at the 8-cm mark.
**Observe** the sounds. **Record** your **observations.**

My observations: _____

_____

## Draw Conclusions

1. **Compare** the sounds you observed in Steps 3 and 4. _____

_____

2. **Compare** the sounds you observed in Steps 5 and 6. _____

_____

3. When was the vibrating part of the rubber band the shortest?

_____

_____

4. **Scientists at Work** Scientists use their observations to help them **infer** the
causes of different things. Use your observations from Steps 5 and 6 to infer

what caused the differences in the sounds. _____

_____

_____

**Investigate Further** Try moving your finger up and down the ruler as you pull on
the rubber band. Can you play a scale? Can you play a tune? What other ways can

you investigate sounds made by the rubber band? _____

_____

_____

_____

_____

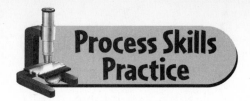

# Infer

When you infer, you use observations to propose causes for things you observe.

## Think About Inferring

**Observe each set of pictures, and infer why each instrument makes the sound it does.**

**A** Banjo makes a low sound.

**B** Banjo with capo makes a higher sound.

**1.** Infer why the banjo in B sounds as it does. _____

_____

**C** Harp makes a loud sound.

**D** Harp makes no sound.

**2.** Infer why the harp in D makes no sound. _____

_____

Harcourt

# Why Do Sounds Differ?

## Lesson Concept

Sound can vary in loudness and in pitch.

## Vocabulary

**loudness** (E68)                                **pitch** (E69)

**Fill in the table below about how and why sounds differ.**

| Property of Sound | Definition | Increase It By | Example of Change Using Specific Instrument |
|---|---|---|---|
| Loudness | | | |
| Pitch | | | |

Harcourt

# Hearing Sounds

## Materials

| | | |
|---|---|---|
| large metal spoon | metal pot | red crayon |

## Activity Procedure

1. Find a playing field with a scoreboard or building at one end. Use a pencil to make a drawing of the playing field on the next page.

2. Walk out onto the playing field. Bang the spoon against the pot once. Wait and **observe** whether or not the sound comes back to you.

3. Use a pencil to **record** on your drawing where you are on the playing field and which way you are facing.

4. Keep moving to new locations on the field and banging the pot until you hear the sound come back to you.

5. **Record** on your drawing where you are on the playing field and which way you are facing each time you bang the pot. Use the red crayon to mark the places where the sound came back to you.

6. Move forward and back. Move from side to side. Each time you move, bang the pot once and wait to see whether or not the sound comes back to you.

7. **Record** on your drawing where you are on the playing field and which way you are facing each time you bang the pot. Use the red crayon to mark the places where the sound came back to you. Make sure your drawing shows at least 20 different positions.

Harcourt

## Draw Conclusions

**1.** Look at your drawing. How many different positions did you show?

_____

At how many different places did the sound come back to you?

_____

**2.** Look at all the places marked in red on your drawing. Do they have anything in

common? _____

_____

**3. Scientists at Work** Each mark that you made on your drawing was a piece of
data. When scientists do investigations, they **gather and record** as much **data**
as they can. All the data helps them draw conclusions. How could you gather

more data in an organized way? _____

_____

_____

**Investigate Further** Move to each of the places on the field where you heard the
sound come back to you. Blow a whistle loudly in each place. Does the sound

come back to you? Why do you think it did or didn't? _____

_____

_____

Harcourt

Name _____

Date _____

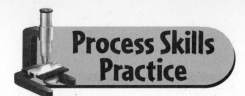

# Gather and Record Data

When you gather and record data, you collect information in an organized way so you can use the information.

## Think About Gathering and Recording Data

Nicki was interested echoes. She decided to gather and record as much data as she could about echoes. The table below shows information she recorded over several days.

| Date | Location | Echo/No Echo | Observations |
|------|----------|--------------|--------------|
| June 2 | outdoor swimming pool | no echo | playing field and much open space near pool, lots of people in pool |
| June 2 | narrow canyon | loud echo | walls of the canyon with little plant growth, day was hot |
| June 3 | large, empty bathroom | echo | no curtains or shades on window, green shower curtain |
| June 4 | large, empty, carpeted living room | soft echo | thick carpet, no furniture, white walls |

**1.** Do you think Nicki did a good job collecting data? Explain. _____

_____

_____

**2.** How could Nicki improve her data? _____

_____

_____

**3.** Where are some other places you think Nicki should collect data? Explain.

_____

_____

_____

Harcourt

Name _____

Date _____

Concept Review

# How Do Sound Waves Travel?

## Lesson Concept

The way sound travels affects how we hear sound.

## Vocabulary

**speed of sound** (E74)     **echo** (E76)     **sonic boom** (E78)

**Answer the questions below about how sound travels.**

1. If you hear a jet flying overhead, where should you look to locate the plane? Why? _____

_____

2. Why do actors in movies who are listening for a train put their ears close to the railroad tracks? _____

_____

_____

3. Why did astronauts who did experiments on the moon communicate with each other using walkie-talkies, even when they were right next to one another?

_____

_____

_____

4. When people build recording studios, they often use soft tiles instead of hard tiles for the ceiling. Why do they do this? _____

_____

5. What causes a sonic boom? _____

_____

_____

_____

# Recognize Vocabulary

Match each term in Column B with its meaning in Column A.

| sound | speed of sound | sound wave | sonic boom |
| pitch | compression | echo | loudness |

**Column A**

_____ 1. moving areas of high and low pressure

_____ 2. a series of vibrations you can hear

_____ 3. a shock wave produced by an object traveling faster than the speed of sound

_____ 4. a measure of the sound energy reaching your ear

_____ 5. a sound reflection

_____ 6. a measure of how high or low a sound is

_____ 7. the speed at which sound waves travel

_____ 8. an area where air is pushed together

**Column B**

**A** compression

**B** echo

**C** loudness

**D** pitch

**E** sonic boom

**F** sound

**G** sound waves

**H** speed of sound

Harcourt

# Chapter 4 • Graphic Organizer for Chapter Concepts

## Electricity and Magnetism

### LESSON 1
### WHAT IS STATIC ELECTRICITY?

Charges that Don't Move

1. Two kinds of charges are _____ and _____ .

2. A charge that does not move is called _____ .

3. When charges are separated on objects, it is the _____ charges that move.

4. The space around a charged object where electric forces act is _____ .

### LESSON 2
### WHAT IS AN ELECTRIC CURRENT?

Moving Charges

5. The flow of charges is called _____ .

6. A _____ is a path for electric current.

7. A _____ adds energy to a circuit. It is also called _____ .

8. Charges move freely through _____ .

9. Charges don't move easily through _____ .

10. The movement of charges is reduced through _____ .

11. A _____ circuit has two or more paths for moving charges.

### LESSON 3
### WHAT IS A MAGNET?

Magnets

12. A magnet attracts material made of _____ .

13. Magnetic forces are strongest at a magnet's _____ .

14. The space near a magnet where magnetic forces act is called the _____ field.

### LESSON 4
### WHAT IS AN ELECTROMAGNET?

Electromagnets

15. Current in a wire produces a _____ field around the wire.

16. If you loop the wire around an _____ , you make an electromagnet.

17. Two ways to make an electromagnet stronger are _____ and _____ .

18. A _____ produces electricity from a magnetic field.

Harcourt

Name _____

Date _____

# Balloons Rubbed with Different Materials

## Materials

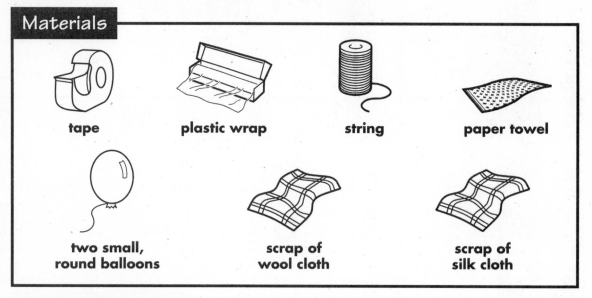

tape

plastic wrap

string

paper towel

two small, round balloons

scrap of wool cloth

scrap of silk cloth

## Activity Procedure

**1** Blow up the balloons, and tie them closed. Use string and tape to hang one balloon from a shelf or table.

**2** Rub the silk all over each balloon. Slowly bring the free balloon near the hanging balloon. **Observe** the hanging balloon. **Record** your observations.

**My observations:** _____

**3** Again rub the silk all over the hanging balloon. Move the silk away. Then slowly bring the silk close to the balloon. **Observe** the hanging balloon, and **record** your observations.

**My observations:** _____

**4** Repeat Steps 2 and 3 separately with the wool, a paper towel, and plastic wrap. **Record** your **observations**.

**My observations:** _____

**5** Rub the silk all over the hanging balloon. Rub the wool all over the free balloon. Slowly bring the free balloon near the hanging balloon. **Observe** the hanging balloon. **Record** your observations.

**My observations:** _____

Harcourt

Name _____

 **Investigate Log**

## Draw Conclusions

1. **Compare** your observations of the two balloons in Step 2 with your observations of a balloon and the material it was rubbed with in Steps 3 and 4.

_____

_____

_____

_____

2. **Compare** your observations of the hanging balloon in Step 2 with your observations of it in Step 5. _____

_____

_____

3. **Scientists at Work** Which of your observations support the **inference** that a force acted on the balloons and materials? Explain your answer.

_____

_____

_____

_____

**Investigate Further** When you rubbed the balloons, you caused a charge to build up. Like charges repel. Opposite charges attract. Review your results for each trial. Tell whether the balloons or material had like charges or opposite charges.

_____

_____

_____

Harcourt

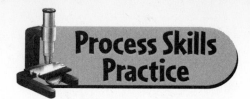

Process Skills Practice

# Infer

You can use observations of how objects move in relation to one another to infer whether or not the objects have electric charge.

## Think About Inferring

On a cold winter day, Lourdes got ready to go to school. She brushed her hair for several minutes. After she brushed her hair, it stuck out and would not lie flat. She walked across the living room carpet and touched the metal doorknob. She got a shock. Her mother explained that her body had built up a charge by walking across the carpet and the shock she experienced was the transfer of that charge to the doorknob.

When she got to school, her teacher did a demonstration with a large, round, metal ball perched on a pedestal. Her teacher called this a Van de Graaff generator. She turned on the generator and asked Lourdes to touch it. Lourdes's hair stuck straight out. Then Lourdes's friend Niles touched her on the shoulder. He felt a shock.

1. Infer why Lourdes's hair stuck out when she combed it. What observations can you use to support this inference? _____

_____

_____

_____

_____

2. Infer why Lourdes's hair stood on end when she touched the Van de Graaff generator. What observations can you use to support this inference?

_____

_____

_____

3. Infer why Niles experienced a shock when he touched Lourdes's shoulder.

_____

_____

Harcourt

Name _____

Date _____

# What Is Static Electricity?

## Lesson Concept

Objects become electrically charged when they gain or lose negative charges.

## Vocabulary

**charge** (E90)     **static electricity** (E90)     **electric field** (E92)

**Answer the questions below about static electricity.**

**1.** What is electric charge? _____

_____

**2.** How can you cause charge to build up on an object? _____

_____

**3.** What is static electricity and why is this name used? _____

_____

_____

**4.** Say you rubbed two balloons with a piece of wool and brought the balloons close to one another. Show the charge buildup on the balloons and what the electric field would look like between them.

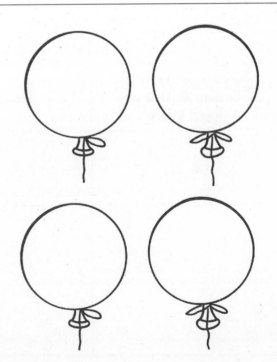

**5.** Suppose you rubbed one balloon with a piece of wool and another balloon with a piece of silk and then brought the two balloons close to one another. Show the charge buildup on the balloons and what the electric field would look like between them.

Harcourt

**Use with page E93.**

# Making a Bulb Light Up

## Materials

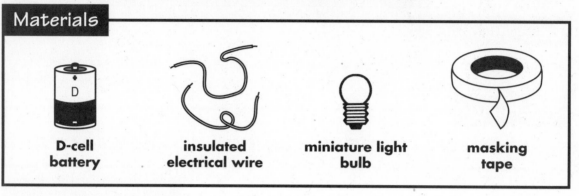

| D-cell battery | insulated electrical wire | miniature light bulb | masking tape |

## Activity Procedure

1. Use the chart below to **record** your **observations**.

2. **Predict** a way to arrange the materials you have been given so that the bulb lights up. Make a drawing to **record** your prediction.

3. Test your prediction. **Record** whether or not the bulb lights up.

4. Continue to work with the bulb, the battery, and the wire. Try different arrangements to get the bulb to light. **Record** the results of each try.

| Predictions and Observations | | |
|---|---|---|
| **Arrangement of Bulb, Battery, and Wire** | **Drawing** | **Observations** |
| | | |
| | | |
| | | |

Harcourt

**Investigate Log**

## Draw Conclusions

**1.** What did you **observe** about the arrangement of materials when the bulb lighted? _____

_____

_____

**2.** What did you **observe** about the arrangement of materials when the bulb did NOT light? _____

_____

**3. Scientists at Work** To find out more about bulbs and batteries, you could **plan and conduct an investigation** of your own. To do that, you need to decide the following: What question do you want to answer? What materials will you need? How will you use the materials? What will you observe?

_____

_____

_____

**Investigate Further** Plan and conduct your investigation.

**My plan:** _____

_____

_____

_____

_____

_____

**My results:** _____

_____

_____

_____

_____

_____

Harcourt

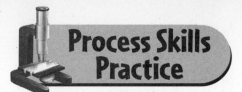

# Plan a Simple Investigation

You can answer questions about electric circuits by planning and conducting simple investigations.

## Think About Planning a Simple Investigation

Jan wants to learn which kinds of batteries will light a medium-sized light bulb like the one in the drawing below. She plans a simple investigation to find out.

1. What materials will Jan need? _____

_____

2. How should Jan set up these materials? _____

_____

_____

_____

3. What should she change in different trials to help her find out what she wants

to learn? _____

_____

4. Make a chart to show how Jan should record her observations.

Harcourt

Name _____

Date _____

# What Is an Electric Current?

## Lesson Concept

Electric current is a flow of charges through a path called a circuit.

## Vocabulary

| | | |
|---|---|---|
| **electric current** (E96) | **circuit** (E96) | **electric cell** (E96) |
| **conductor** (E97) | **insulator** (E97) | **resistor** (E97) |
| **series circuit** (E98) | **parallel circuit** (E98) | |

Match each term in Column A with its meaning or its picture in Column B.

**Column A**

_____ **1.** circuit

_____ **2.** conductor

_____ **3.** electric cell

_____ **4.** electric current

_____ **5.** insulator

_____ **6.** parallel circuit

_____ **7.** resistor

_____ **8.** series circuit

**Column B**

**A** a path made for an electric current

**B** a material current cannot pass through easily

**C** a flow of electric charges

**D** a material that resists but does not stop the flow of current

**E** a material that current can pass through easily

**F**    **G**    **H**

**9.** Label the conductor **A**, the switch **B**, the electric cell **C**, the resistors **D**, and the type of circuit in this diagram. Use arrows to show where the current flows in the diagram.

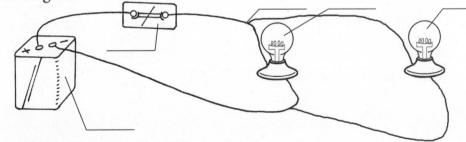

Circuit type: _____

Harcourt

Name _____

Date _____

# A Compass

## Materials

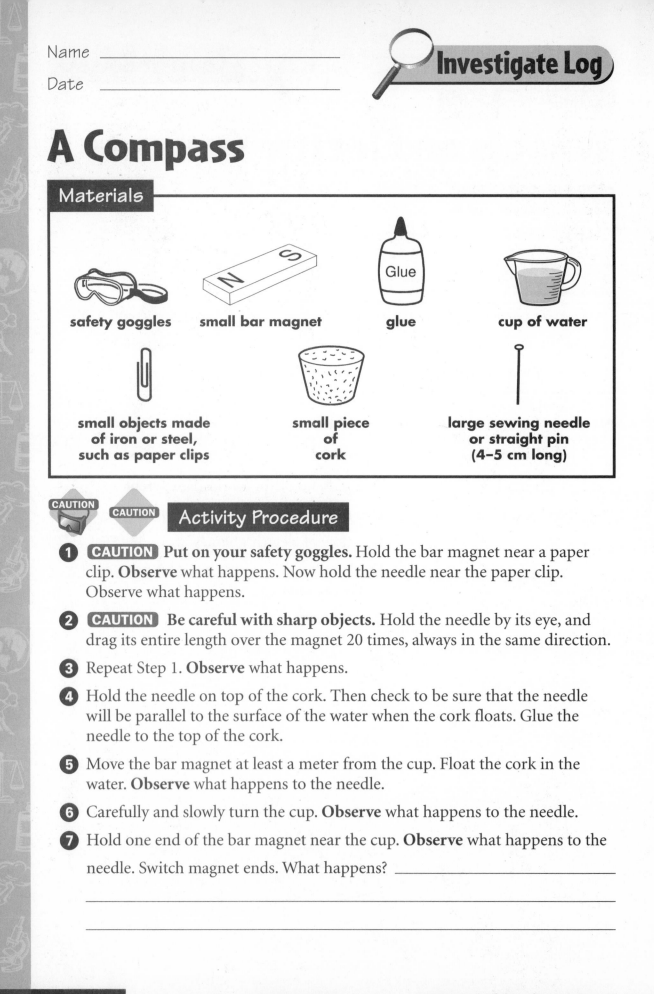

safety goggles          small bar magnet          glue          cup of water

small objects made
of iron or steel,
such as paper clips

small piece
of
cork

large sewing needle
or straight pin
(4–5 cm long)

⚠️ CAUTION  ⚠️ CAUTION    **Activity Procedure**

**❶** **CAUTION** **Put on your safety goggles.** Hold the bar magnet near a paper clip. **Observe** what happens. Now hold the needle near the paper clip. Observe what happens.

**❷** **CAUTION** **Be careful with sharp objects.** Hold the needle by its eye, and drag its entire length over the magnet 20 times, always in the same direction.

**❸** Repeat Step 1. **Observe** what happens.

**❹** Hold the needle on top of the cork. Then check to be sure that the needle will be parallel to the surface of the water when the cork floats. Glue the needle to the top of the cork.

**❺** Move the bar magnet at least a meter from the cup. Float the cork in the water. **Observe** what happens to the needle.

**❻** Carefully and slowly turn the cup. **Observe** what happens to the needle.

**❼** Hold one end of the bar magnet near the cup. **Observe** what happens to the needle. Switch magnet ends. What happens? _____

_____

_____

Harcourt

## Draw Conclusions

1. Describe what happened when you floated the cork with the needle in the water. What happened when you turned the cup? _____

_____

_____

2. What happened when you brought the bar magnet near the floating needle?

_____

_____

_____

3. **Scientists at Work** What **hypothesis** can you make based on your observations of the needle? _____

_____

_____

_____

What predictions can you make by using your hypothesis? _____

_____

_____

**Investigate Further Plan and carry out a simple investigation** to test one of your predictions from Question 3, above.

**My plan:** _____

_____

_____

**My observations:** _____

_____

_____

**My results:** _____

_____

_____

Harcourt

Name _____

Date _____

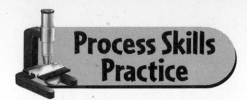

# Hypothesize

Making a hypothesis involves using observations to come up
with an explanation that you can test with experiments.

## Think About Hypothesizing

Aziz noticed that a strong bar magnet he was playing with attracted a small plastic
car. He could use the magnet to pull the car around on the floor.

1. Based on this observation, what hypothesis might Aziz make about the magnet
   and plastic car? _____

   _____

   _____

2. Pick a hypothesis from Question 1. Describe how Aziz might test this

   hypothesis. _____

   _____

   _____

3. If the hypothesis tested in Question 2 did not turn out to be true, how could
   Aziz change it to fit the new information? How could he test his new

   hypothesis? _____

   _____

   _____

   _____

   _____

   _____

Harcourt

Name _____

Date _____

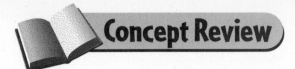
**Concept Review**

# What Is a Magnet?

## Lesson Concept

A magnet is an object that attracts certain materials.

### Vocabulary

**magnet** (E102)　　**magnetic pole** (E102)　　**magnetic field** (E103)

**Answer the questions below about magnets.**

**1.** Complete the drawing of the bar magnet by labeling the poles and drawing the magnetic lines of force around the magnet.

**2.** Describe what would happen if you held up the *S* pole of a bar magnet near the *N* pole of the magnet shown above. In the space below, draw the magnets, label the poles, and show the resulting shape of the magnetic field near the magnets.

_____

**3.** How does a compass work to help people tell directions?

_____

_____

_____

_____

Harcourt

Name _____

Date _____

# How Magnets and Electricity Can Interact

## Materials

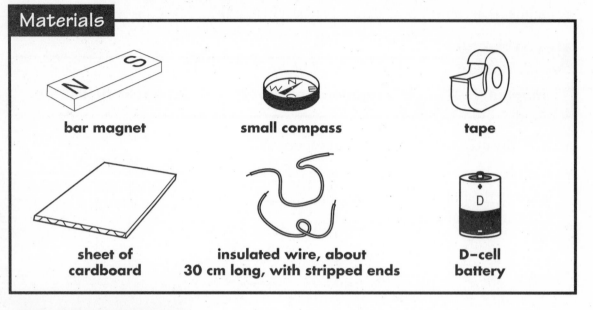

bar magnet

small compass

tape

sheet of cardboard

insulated wire, about 30 cm long, with stripped ends

D-cell battery

## Activity Procedure

**1** Try several positions of the magnet and compass. **Record** your **observations** of how the magnet affects the compass needle.

**My observations:** _____

_____

**2** Place the compass flat on the cardboard so the needle is lined up with north. Tape the middle third of the insulated wire onto the cardboard in a north-south line.

**3** Tape one end of the wire to the flat end of a D-cell battery. Tape the battery to the cardboard.

**4** Without moving the cardboard, put the compass on the taped-down part of the wire.

**5** Touch the free end of the wire to the (+) end of the battery for a few seconds. **Observe** the compass needle. Repeat this step several more times. **Record** your observations.

**My observations:** _____

_____

Harcourt

**6** Carefully remove the taped wire.
Place the compass underneath the wire so that both line up along a north-south line. **Predict** what will happen if you repeat Step 5.

**My prediction:** _____

_____

**7** Repeat Step 5. **Record** your observations.

**My observations:** _____

_____

## Draw Conclusions

**1. Compare** your observations in Step 5 with those in Step 7. Was your prediction accurate? Explain. _____

_____

_____

_____

_____

**2.** Using what you know about compasses in magnetic fields, what can you **infer** about currents in wires? _____

_____

_____

_____

**3. Scientists at Work** Just as you predicted what would happen in Step 7, scientists often **predict** the outcome of an experiment based on their observations and inferences. Based on your observations, what would you predict will happen in the experiment if the current is made to move in the opposite direction? _____

_____

**Investigate Further** Test your **prediction**. Remove the battery from the cardboard. Turn it so that its ends are pointing in the opposite direction.

Attach the wire again. **Record** your **observations.** _____

_____

_____

Harcourt

Name _____

Date _____

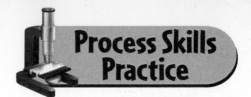

# Predict

When you predict, you use what you know from observations you have made in the past to say what you think will happen in an experiment.

## Think About Predicting

Gustav was testing the strength of the magnetic field near different magnets. He had a horseshoe magnet, a bar magnet, and a needle that he magnetized using the bar magnet. Gustav predicted that the horseshoe magnet would pick up the most paper clips, and the magnetized needle would pick up the least. After he made his predictions, Gustav tested to see how many paper clips each magnet would pick up.

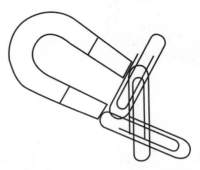

| Magnet | Gustav's Prediction of the Number of Paper Clips It Would Pick Up | Actual Number of Paper Clips Picked Up |
|---|---|---|
| Horseshoe magnet | 30 | 100 |
| Bar magnet | 20 | 57 |
| Needle magnetized by rubbing it against the bar ten times | 2 | 1 |

1. The table above shows Gustav's predictions and his results. What was correct about Gustav's predictions? _____

_____

2. Gustav predicted that if he rubbed the needle against the magnet 50 times, he would be able to pick up five paper clips. Do you think this is a good prediction? Explain. _____

_____

3. Gustav tested his prediction, and he found that after rubbing the needle 50 times, it would still pick up only one paper clip. Was your prediction correct?

_____

Harcourt

# What Is an Electromagnet?

## Lesson Concept

Electricity and magnetism can interact to produce electromagnets.

## Vocabulary

**electromagnet** (E109)

**Answer the questions below about electromagnetism.**

**1.** Describe one way to make an electromagnet. _____

_____

_____

**2.** How is an electromagnet different from a bar magnet? _____

_____

_____

_____

**Which picture shows the motor and which shows the generator?**
**Briefly tell how each works.**

**3.** _____

_____

_____

_____

_____

**4.** _____

_____

_____

_____

Harcourt

Name _____

Date _____

# Recognize Vocabulary

**Read each sentence below. If the sentence is correct, write *True* on the line. If the sentence is incorrect, write *False* on the line.**

_____ **1.** Charge is the measure of extra positive or negative particles an object has.

_____ **2.** A circuit is a path made for a magnetic field.

_____ **3.** Electric current can pass easily through a conductor.

_____ **4.** An electric cell supplies energy to move charges through an electric field.

_____ **5.** A flow of electromagnets is called an electric current.

_____ **6.** An electric field is the space around an object where electric forces occur.

_____ **7.** An electromagnet is a wire wrapped around a solid core and connected in a circuit.

_____ **8.** An insulator is a material that electric cells cannot pass through.

_____ **9.** A magnet attracts certain materials, including plastics.

_____ **10.** A magnetic field is the space around an object where magnets form.

_____ **11.** Magnetic poles are the ends of a magnet where the magnetic field is strongest.

_____ **12.** The current in a parallel circuit travels in only one path.

_____ **13.** A resistor is material that increases the flow of electric charges.

_____ **14.** The current in a series circuit travels in more than one path.

_____ **15.** Static electricity stays on an object.

Harcourt

**Use with pages E88–E113.**

# Chapter 1 • Graphic Organizer for Chapter Concepts

## Motion—Forces at Work

### LESSON 1
### MOTION

Definition _____

Measured as _____

which involves _____

### LESSON 2
### FORCE

Definition _____

Causes _____
_____

Measured in _____

### LESSON 3
### FORCES IN NATURE

Force        What It Does

1. _____  _____

2. _____  _____

3. _____  _____

4. _____  _____

Harcourt

Name _____

Date _____

# Giving Directions

## Materials

paper – pencil

## Activity Procedure

**1** Choose a place in the school, such as a water fountain or an exit door. A person going there should have to make several turns. Tell your teacher the place you chose.

**2** After your teacher has approved your place, start walking to it. As you walk, **record** where and how you are moving. For example, you might include the distance you walk, about how long it takes for each part of the trip, where you turn, and any landmarks you use to tell where you are.

**My movements:** _____

_____

**3** Go back to your classroom. On a separate sheet of paper, write directions to the place you chose. Use your notes to add details about time, distance, and position. Don't name the place on the directions page. Give the directions to a classmate and ask him or her to follow them.

**4** When your partner comes back, talk about any problems he or she had with your directions. Underline the parts of the directions that caused the problems.

**5** Walk with your partner as he or she follows the directions again. Decide together how to make the directions clearer. **Record** the reasons for any changes.

**My reasons:** _____

_____

**6** Switch roles with your partner and repeat Steps 1–6.

Harcourt

## Draw Conclusions

**1.** How did your partner know where to start following the directions?

_____

_____

_____

**2.** How did your partner know how far to walk? _____

_____

_____

How did your partner know which direction to walk, and where to turn?

_____

_____

**3. Scientists at Work** Directions **communicate** the way to get from one place to another. **Compare** your directions to the procedure of an experiment.

_____

_____

_____

**Investigate Further** Using your notes and directions, draw a map showing the way to the place you chose. Trade maps with a new partner. Is the map easier to use than written directions? Explain your answer. _____

_____

_____

_____

_____

# Communicate

When you describe an experiment, you are communicating. Clear communication is important for others to understand your experiment and repeat it.

## Think About Communicating

Ann and Carl did an experiment to find the speed of a ball that rolled down a ramp. Ann described their experiment so that Josh could repeat it.

---

**Purpose:** To measure the speed of a ball rolling on the floor.

**Materials:** 3 books, tennis ball, masking tape, stopwatch, meterstick

**Procedure:**

1. At one end of a long hallway, I used three books to make a ramp.

2. I held the ball at the top of the ramp. Carl took the stopwatch and the masking tape to the other end of the hallway.

3. Carl signaled me and started the stopwatch. I saw the signal and released the ball.

4. Carl observed the ball and stopped the stopwatch when the ball stopped rolling. He marked the ball's position with masking tape.

5. I measured the distance the ball traveled. I divided the distance the ball traveled by the time it took, to figure out the speed of the ball.

**Results:** The ball traveled 2.65 meters in 7 seconds.
The ball's speed was 0.38 meters per second.

---

1. In describing her experiment, how did Ann divide her report into parts?

   _____

2. What questions should Josh ask Ann about the experiment? _____

   _____

   _____

   _____

3. How would you rewrite parts of Ann's experiment to make the directions

   clearer? _____

   _____

   _____

Harcourt

# What Is Motion?

## Lesson Concept

Motion is any change in an object's position.

## Vocabulary

**position** (F6)          **motion** (F6)          **frame of reference** (F7)

**relative motion** (F7)          **speed** (F8)

**Answer the questions below about motion.**

**Postcard A**

**Postcard B**

1. Observe Postcard A. Suppose you are the runner looking back. How would you describe the position of the other runner? _____

2. Observe Postcard B. Suppose you are in the crowd, watching the race. How do you know the runners are in motion? _____
   _____

3. What is the frame of reference of Postcard A? How can you tell?
   _____
   _____

4. What is the frame of reference of Postcard B? How can you tell?
   _____
   _____

5. The winner of this race ran 1500 meters in 5 minutes and 22 seconds. What was the winner's speed in m/sec? Show all of your work. _____
   _____

Harcourt

# Pairs of Forces Acting on Objects

## Materials

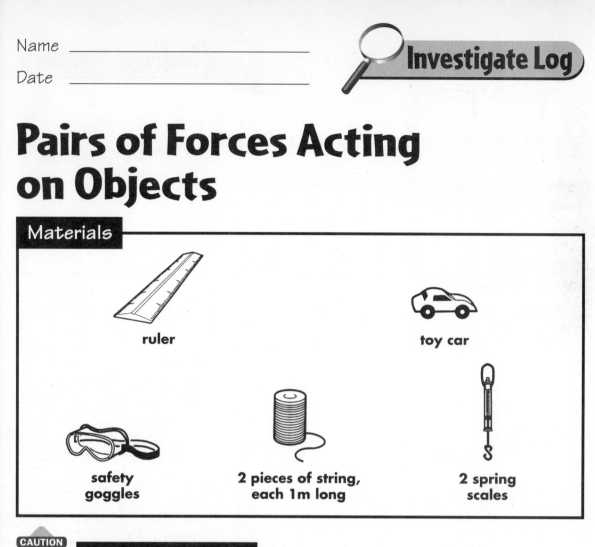

ruler

toy car

safety goggles

2 pieces of string, each 1m long

2 spring scales

## CAUTION  Activity Procedure

**1** **CAUTION** **Wear safety goggles to protect your eyes. The spring scale hooks or string may slip loose and fly up**. Work with a partner. Tie the ends of each string to the toy car. Pull on the string to make sure it won't come off easily. Attach a spring scale to each loop of string.

**2** With a partner, try different ways and directions of pulling on the spring scales attached to the toy car.

**3** **Plan a simple investigation.** Your goal is to **describe** how the toy car moves when two spring scales pull it at the same time. Plan to include a chart and a diagram to **record** your data and **observations.**

**4** With your partner, carry out the investigation you planned.

Name _____

## Draw Conclusions

1. How did pulling in different directions affect the toy car? _____

_____

_____

_____

2. How did pulling in the same direction affect the toy car? _____

_____

_____

_____

3. **Scientists at Work**  Scientists use what they know to help them **plan and conduct investigations**. What knowledge did you use to help you plan and

conduct this investigation? _____

_____

_____

**Investigate Further**  What would happen if you attached a third piece of string and another spring scale to the car? **Plan and conduct an investigation** to find out. Can you find a way to have three people pull without moving the car?

Explain your answer. _____

_____

_____

_____

_____

Harcourt

Name _____

Date _____

# Plan and Conduct an Investigation

Planning and conducting an investigation can help you answer questions about changes in motion.

## Think About Planning and Conducting an Investigation

Langston wants to plan and conduct an investigation that will help him learn how changing the height of a ramp affects how a toy car moves.

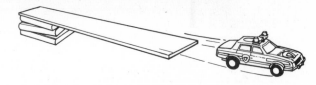

1. To plan an investigation, Langston first needs to pose a question, starting with what he wants to learn. What question do you think Langston should pose?

   _____

   _____

2. Identify what Langston should measure, change, and keep the same to answer his question, and how he should do each of these things. What should

   Langston measure? _____

   _____

   What should Langston change? _____

   What should Langston keep the same? _____

   _____

3. Draw or describe in words Langston's investigation. _____

   _____

   _____

   _____

   _____

4. What knowledge did you use to come up with ideas for Langston's

   investigation? _____

   _____

   _____

Harcourt

**Use with page F11.**

# What Effects Do Forces Have on Objects?

## Lesson Concept

Forces can affect how objects move.

## Vocabulary

**force** (F12)          **acceleration** (F14)          **newton** (F17)

**1.** Define *force*, and name the unit used to measure forces.

_____

**2.** Define acceleration, and tell how acceleration is related to force.

_____

_____

**3.** List two ways you can increase acceleration. _____

_____

_____

**4.** Below are pictures of forces. Use arrows to draw the forces in each picture. The lengths of the arrows should indicate the relative sizes of the forces.

Harcourt

# Forces on a Sliding Box

## Materials

**shoe box**          **spring scale**          **books**

## Activity Procedure

**1** Use the table below to **record** your **observations**.

**2** Put the hook of the spring scale through the two openings on the end of the box. Place several books in the box.

**3** Use the spring scale to slowly drag the box across the top of the desk or table. Be sure to pull with the spring scale straight out from the side of the box. Practice this step several times until you can pull the box at a steady, slow speed.

**4** When you are ready, **measure** the force of your pull as you drag the box. **Record** the force measurement and the surface on which you dragged the box. **Observe** the texture of the surface.

**5** Repeat Steps 3 and 4, dragging the box across other surfaces, such as the classroom floor, carpet, tile, and cement. **Predict** the force needed to drag the box on each surface.

| Surface | Predicted Force | Force |
|---------|-----------------|-------|
|         |                 |       |
|         |                 |       |
|         |                 |       |
|         |                 |       |
|         |                 |       |
|         |                 |       |

Harcourt

Name _____

## Draw Conclusions

1. In the table below, list the forces you used in order from the smallest to the largest.

| Force Used | Surface |
|---|---|
|  |  |
|  |  |
|  |  |

What was the least amount of force you used? _____

_____

_____

2. In your new table, write the name of each surface next to the force you used on it. On which surface did you use the greatest amount of force?

_____

_____

3. How did a surface affect the force needed to drag the shoe box across it?

_____

_____

4. **Scientists at Work** After scientists gather data, they often put it in some kind of order to help them understand their results. How did putting your data in

   **order** help you in this investigation? _____

_____

**Investigate Further** **Predict** how much force it would take to pull the shoe box across a patch of ice. If possible, find a place and test your prediction.

_____

_____

Harcourt

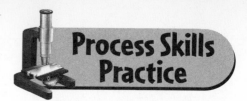

# Order

You put data in order when you rank the data from lowest to highest.

## Think About Ordering

Jaya read that friction slows moving objects and can make them stop. She tested different materials to see how well each could stop a rolling golf ball. She rolled a set of golf balls, one at a time, down a short ramp onto different surfaces and measured how far they rolled before they stopped. For each of the surfaces, she averaged the distances the golf balls rolled. The table shows her data.

| Material | Average Distance |
|---|---|
| Corrugated cardboard | 41 cm |
| Thin-pile carpet | 32 cm |
| Thick-pile carpet | 22 cm |
| Plastic with small spikes (under-side of carpet protector) | 10 cm |
| Smooth plastic (carpet protector) | 115 cm |
| Carpet pad (carpet side) | 52 cm |

1. Jaya is trying to find the material that will stop rolling golf balls the fastest. To order the materials she tested from best to worst, should she start with the highest measurement or the lowest measurement? Explain.

_____

_____

2. Order the materials from the best material to stop a rolling golf ball to the worst.

| Material | Average Distance |
|---|---|
|  |  |
|  |  |
|  |  |
|  |  |
|  |  |
|  |  |

Harcourt

**Use with page F21.**

Name _____

Date _____

**Concept Review**

# What Are Some Forces in Nature?

## Lesson Concept

Gravity, friction, the electromagnetic force, and the strong nuclear force are some forces in nature.

## Vocabulary

**gravity** (F22)          **weight** (F23)          **friction** (26)

**Answer the questions below about forces.**

**1.** Define *gravity*, and write three facts about gravity. _____

_____

_____

_____

_____

**2.** What is weight? Why does weight vary on different planets? _____

_____

_____

**3.** What is friction, and how is it useful to you? _____

_____

_____

**Label the parts of the atom and the forces between the different parts.**

**4.** _____

**5.** _____

**6.** _____

**7.** _____ force

**8.** _____ force

Harcourt

**Vocabulary Review**

# Recognize Vocabulary

Match each term in Column B with its meaning in Column A.

| | | |
|---|---|---|
| position | motion | frame of reference |
| relative motion | speed | force |
| newton | acceleration | gravity |
| weight | friction | |

## Column A

_____ 1. any change of position

_____ 2. the measure of the force of gravity on an object

_____ 3. a push or a pull

_____ 4. a certain place, described in comparison to another place

_____ 5. a change in the speed or direction of an object's motion

_____ 6. the force that keeps objects that are touching each other from sliding past each other easily

_____ 7. all the things around you that you can sense and use to describe motion

_____ 8. the metric unit of force

_____ 9. a measure of an object's change in position during a unit of time

_____ 10. motion described in relation to a frame of reference

_____ 11. a force that pulls objects toward each other

## Column B

**A** acceleration

**B** force

**C** frame of reference

**D** friction

**E** gravity

**F** motion

**G** newton

**H** position

**I** relative motion

**J** speed

**K** weight

Harcourt

Chapter 2 • Graphic Organizer for Chapter Concepts

## Simple Machines

### LESSON 1
### SIMPLE MACHINES

Types _____

_____

_____

Lever _____

_____

effort force _____

resulting force _____

Example _____

_____

_____

### LESSON 2
### SIMPLE MACHINES
### THAT TURN

Fixed Pulley _____

Description _____

_____

How It Works _____

_____

Movable Pulley _____

Description _____

_____

How It Works _____

Wheel and Axle _____

Description _____

How It Works _____

_____

### LESSON 3
### INCLINED PLANES

Inclined Plane _____

Description _____

_____

How It Works _____

_____

Screw _____

Description _____

_____

How It Works _____

Wedge _____

Description _____

_____

How It Works _____

# Experimenting with a Lever

## Materials

2 wooden rulers    2 identical rubber bands, long    safety goggles

## Activity Procedure

**CAUTION**

1 **CAUTION** **Put on your safety goggles.** Put a rubber band 2 cm from each end of the ruler. One band should be at the 2-cm mark, and the other should be at the 28-cm mark.

| Finger Position | Observations | Length of Rubber Band on 2-cm Mark | Length of Rubber Band on 28-cm Mark |
|---|---|---|---|
| 15-cm mark | | | |
| 17-cm mark | | | |
| 19-cm mark | | | |
| 21-cm mark | | | |

Harcourt

Name _____

**2** Have a partner lift the ruler by holding the rubber bands. Place your index finger at the 15-cm mark, and press down just enough to stretch the rubber bands. Your partner should lift hard enough on both rubber bands to keep the ruler level.

**3** **Observe** the positions of all parts of the ruler. Have a third person use the other ruler to **measure** the lengths of the two bands. **Record** your **observations** and measurements in the chart on WB258.

**4** Move your finger to the 17-cm mark. Your partner should lift hard enough on each rubber band to keep the ruler level. Again **observe** the rubber bands, **measure** their lengths, and **record** your **observations** and measurements.

**5** Repeat Step 4, this time with your finger at the 19-cm mark and then the 21-cm mark.

## Draw Conclusions

1. Describe what happened to the ruler each time you moved your finger away from the center of it. _____

_____

2. **Compare** the ruler and rubber bands to a seesaw. What was the ruler? What were the forces of the rubber bands? _____

_____

_____

3. **Scientists at Work** Look at the **measurements** you recorded. How do they support your other observations? Is there a pattern? _____

_____

_____

_____

**Investigate Further** For the same ruler setup, **predict** what will happen if you put your finger on the 9-cm mark. Try it and see if your prediction is correct.

_____

_____

Harcourt

Name _____

Date _____

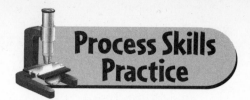

# Measure

You measure when you make observations and comparisons using numbers.

## Think About Measuring

Below are pictures of people on a seesaw. The bar that holds up the seesaw is called the fulcrum. Use a ruler to measure the distance in centimeters between the fulcrum and each end of the seesaw. Record your measurements in the chart below.

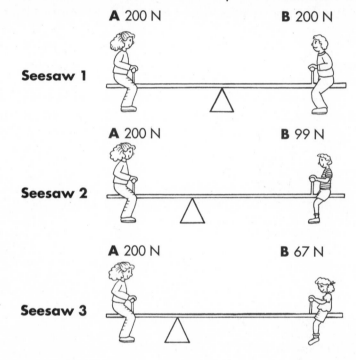

| Seesaw | Distance from A to Fulcrum | Weight of A in Newtons | Distance from B to Fulcrum | Weight of B in Newtons |
|--------|----------------------------|------------------------|----------------------------|------------------------|
| 1 | | 200 N | | 200 N |
| 2 | | 200 N | | 99 N |
| 3 | | 200 N | | 67 N |

What relationship do you see between the distances of the people from the

fulcrum and the people's weights? _____

_____

Harcourt

Name _____

Date _____

# How Does a Lever Help Us Do Work?

## Lesson Concept

A lever is a simple machine that can change the size or direction of a force.

## Vocabulary

**simple machine** (F38)   **lever** (F38)   **fulcrum** (F38)

**effort force** (F38)   **work** (F42)

**Answer the questions below about levers.**

1. What is the scientific definition of work? Write the formula for work.

_____

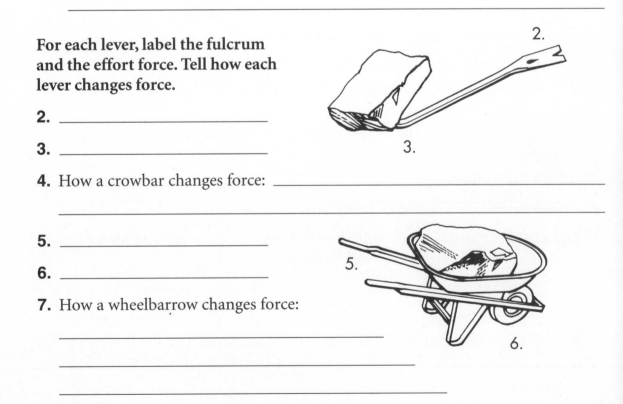

For each lever, label the fulcrum and the effort force. Tell how each lever changes force.

2. _____

3. _____

4. How a crowbar changes force: _____

_____

5. _____

6. _____

7. How a wheelbarrow changes force:

_____

_____

Harcourt

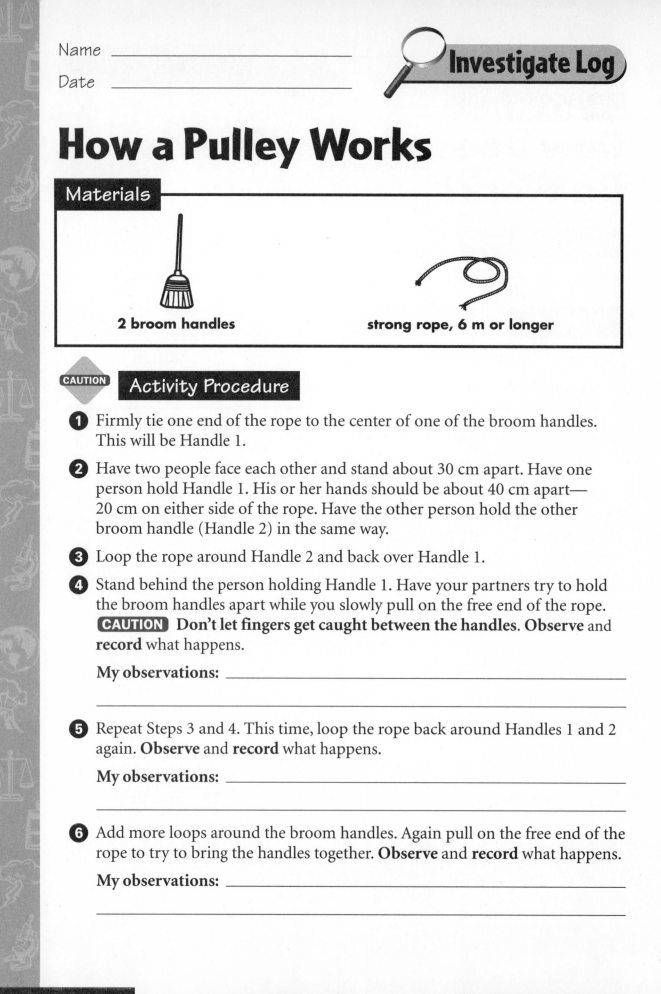
# How a Pulley Works

## Materials

2 broom handles

strong rope, 6 m or longer

CAUTION  ## Activity Procedure

**1** Firmly tie one end of the rope to the center of one of the broom handles. This will be Handle 1.

**2** Have two people face each other and stand about 30 cm apart. Have one person hold Handle 1. His or her hands should be about 40 cm apart—20 cm on either side of the rope. Have the other person hold the other broom handle (Handle 2) in the same way.

**3** Loop the rope around Handle 2 and back over Handle 1.

**4** Stand behind the person holding Handle 1. Have your partners try to hold the broom handles apart while you slowly pull on the free end of the rope. **CAUTION** **Don't let fingers get caught between the handles. Observe** and **record** what happens.

**My observations:** _____

_____

**5** Repeat Steps 3 and 4. This time, loop the rope back around Handles 1 and 2 again. **Observe** and **record** what happens.

**My observations:** _____

_____

**6** Add more loops around the broom handles. Again pull on the free end of the rope to try to bring the handles together. **Observe** and **record** what happens.

**My observations:** _____

_____

Harcourt

Name _____

## Draw Conclusions

1. **Compare** your observations in Steps 4, 5, and 6. Which way of looping the rope made it hardest to pull the handles together? Which way made it easiest?

   _____

   _____

   _____

2. Reread the description of a pulley in the Activity Purpose. What in this

   investigation worked as wheels do? _____

   _____

3. **Scientists at Work** How did the handles and rope change your effort force? **Compare** this to how levers work. How is it like levers? How is it different?

   _____

   _____

   _____

   _____

**Investigate Further** Attach a spring scale to the free end of the rope and repeat the investigation. Use one, two, three, and four loops around the broom handles. **Record** your results in a table. Then make a graph that **compares** the force needed

for each number of loops. _____

_____

_____

_____

Harcourt

Name _____

Date _____

Process Skills Practice

# Compare

Comparing involves noticing how things are alike and how they are different.

Tyrone looks in his father's toolbox. He notices two different screwdrivers.

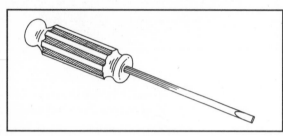

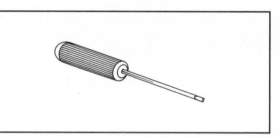

**Screwdriver A**                     **Screwdriver B**

**1.** How are these tools alike? _____

_____

**2.** How are these tools different? _____

_____

**3.** Which screwdriver could Tyrone use to unscrew a door from its hinges?

_____

**4.** Which screwdriver could Tyrone use to take apart a watch? _____

_____

**5.** Why couldn't Tyrone switch the tools for the jobs in Questions 3 and 4?

_____

_____

_____

_____

Name _____

Date _____

# How Do a Wheel and Axle and a Pulley Help Us Do Work?

### Lesson Concept

A wheel and axle and a pulley are simple machines that can change the size or direction of forces.

### Vocabulary

| | |
|---|---|
| **pulley** (F46) | **wheel and axle** (F48) |

**Look at each picture and answer the questions.**

1. What kind of simple machine is shown?

   _____

2. How does this machine help you do work?

   _____

   _____

3. What kind of simple machine is shown?

   _____

4. How does this machine help you do work?

   _____

   _____

   _____

5. What kind of simple machines are put

   together to form this system? _____

   _____

   _____

6. How does this system help you do work? _____

   _____

   _____

Harcourt

**Use with page F49.**

# Make an Archimedes' Screw

## Materials

**round wooden pole, such as a piece of a broom handle, 20 cm long**

**large pan of water or sink that can be filled with water**

**length of rubber or plastic hose, about 40–50 cm long**

**marker**

**6 strong rubber bands**

**meterstick or metric ruler**

## Activity Procedure

1. Use the meterstick and marker to divide the pole into five equal sections.

2. Use a rubber band to hold the hose to one end of the pole. The band should not be so tight that it closes off the hose, but it should be tight enough to hold the hose in place.

3. Wind the hose around the pole in a spiral so that it passes over your marks. Use a rubber band to hold the top of the hose in place. Put two or three more bands around the hose and pole so that nothing slips. Wiggle the hose around so the ends open at right angles to the length of the pole. You have built an Archimedes' screw.

4. Put the nail end of the Archimedes' screw in the large pan or sink of water so the device rests on the head of the nail and makes a low angle with the bottom of the pan. Make sure both ends of the screw are over the pan. Turn the Archimedes' screw clockwise 12 times. Now turn the screw in the other direction 12 times. **Observe** what happens.

Harcourt

Name _____

## Draw Conclusions

1. What happened when you turned the Archimedes' screw the first time?

   What happened the second time? _____

   _____

   _____

2. A screw is a type of inclined plane, a flat sloping surface. A ramp is an example of an inclined plane. Where was the inclined plane in the model you made?

   _____

   _____

3. **Scientists at Work**  The Archimedes' screw you built is not a completely useful tool. The screw is hard to turn, and there are easier ways to move water. But it is useful as a **model**. It shows how the machine works. Why might it help to make a small model before building a full-size machine?

   _____

   _____

   _____

**Investigate Further**  There are many inclined planes around you. Select one day to see how many ramps and screws you can find at school and at home. Make a list of those you find. Tell how each helps people do work.

_____

_____

_____

_____

_____

Harcourt

Name _____

Date _____

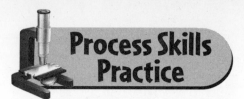

# Make a Model

Making a small model of a simple machine can help you investigate ways to improve the real thing.

## Think About Making a Model

Jasper is moving from his apartment to a house. He asked his friends to help him move. He had an idea to make moving more easy. He thought they could use a pulley system to move boxes up an inclined plane and into a truck, instead of carrying the boxes to the truck. He knew that most ramps are made of surfaces that are not slippery, so that people can walk on them without falling. He wanted to make a slippery surface for his ramp so that the boxes would slide up easily. He decided to make a small model to test different surfaces.

**1.** If you were Jasper, how would you make your model? Draw a picture, labeling the parts and indicating the size of each part.

 

**2.** What kinds of materials could Jasper test? _____

_____

_____

**3.** What could Jasper use as a load to pull up his model ramp? _____

_____

_____

**4.** What could Jasper measure to test the different surfaces? _____

_____

_____

_____

**5.** How could Jasper decide which surface worked the best? _____

_____

_____

Harcourt

# How Do Some Other Simple Machines Help Us Do Work?

**Lesson Concept**

Inclined planes, screws, and wedges are simple machines that help us do work.

**Vocabulary**

| | | |
|---|---|---|
| **inclined plane** (F52) | **screw** (F54) | **wedge** (F56) |

**Match the pictures to the captions, and complete the captions.**

| A | B | C |
|---|---|---|

**1.** Inclined plane _____ helps us do work by _____

_____

_____

**2.** Screw _____ helps us do work by _____

_____

**3.** Wedge _____ helps us do work by _____

_____

_____

**4.** What is the relationship among the three simple machines pictured?

_____

# Recognize Vocabulary

| simple machine | lever | fulcrum | work |
| inclined plane | effort force | wedge | screw |
| wheel and axle | pulley | | |

**Fill in the blanks with the letters of the correct vocabulary terms. Rearrange the circled letters to answer the question below.**

1. lever, wheel and axle, pulley, inclined plane, screw, and wedge

    _ _ _ ◯ _ _    _ _ _ _ _ _ _ _

2. a wheel with a rope or chain fitted around it    _ _ ◯ _ _ _

3. a flat surface with one end higher than the other

    _ _ _ _ _ ◯ _ _ _ ◯ _ _ _ _

4. What is done when a force moves an object across a distance    _ _ _ ◯

5. two inclined planes placed back to back    ◯ _ _ _ _

6. the force you place on a simple machine

    _ _ _ ◯ _ _    _ _ ◯ _ _ _ _

7. a large wheel attached to a smaller wheel or rod

    _ ◯ _ _ _    _ _ _    _ _ _ _

8. the result of wrapping an inclined plane around a pole    ◯ _ _ _ _

9. a bar that turns around a fixed point    _ _ _ ◯ _

10. a fixed point around which a lever moves    _ _ _ _ _ ◯ _

What do simple machines do?

_ _ _ _ _ _ _ _ _ _ _ _

Harcourt